Christopher W. Tremblay presents

Walt's Pilgrimage
A Journey in the Life of Walter Elias Disney

North American Edition

**The Original Place-Based
Biographical Journey of Walt Disney**

Developed in 2014 through WMU's Study in the States

Designs and Photographs
Cover Design by Kevin Robert Ryan.
State/Province/Country Maps Designed by Kevin Robert Ryan.
Icons Designed by Chelsey Miller.
Original passport stamp designed by Maya Sheth.
Photos contained in this book were taken by the author, unless otherwise noted.
Author photo on back cover by Lifetouch.

Map silhouettes courtesy of www.supercoloring.com
Authors: Bob Comix, Natasha Sinegina, et al.
License: Creative Commons Attribution-Share Alike 4.0 License

Permissions
Permission to use the Walt Disney Hometown Museum logo was granted in writing by Peter Whitehead on June 19, 2017. Permission to use the WMU Study in the States logo was granted in writing by Dean Gary Bischof on June 24, 2017. Smoke Tree Ranch logo courtesy of Smoke Tree Ranch and used with written permission. Permission to use the Walt Disney Family Museum logo was granted in writing by Caitlin Moneypenny-Johnston on August 22, 2017. Permission to use the Gilmore Car Museum logo was granted in writing by Fred Colgren on August 18, 2017.

Font
Internal font used is Ebrima.

Disclaimer
This information is subject to change at any time. It was up-to-date at the time of printing. Check websites provided and contact sites as you plan your adventures.

Printed in the United States of America
First Edition: June 2018 printing (3.0)
ISBN 978-1548208059

Dedication

Dedicated to Madeline and Gerard Tremblay,
my parents, who introduced me to
Mickey Mouse and Walt Disney World
at a very young age.

Thank you for always supporting my
lifelong passion for all things Disney.
Ears 2 U!

"I love the nostalgic myself. I hope we never lose some of the things of the past."
-Walt Disney

"Always, as you travel, assimilate the sounds and sights of the world."
-Walt Disney

This book unites those two statements
made by Walt Disney as it is designed for the travelers
who wish to step into history and walk in his life.

Both quotations come from the
1994 *Walt Disney Famous Quotes* publication
(p. 78 and 94).

Table of Contents

Inspiration for this Book

In December 2013, two Disney moments collided in my world: the Kickstarter campaign for The Walt Disney Birthplace and the Treasures of the Walt Disney Archives exhibit in Chicago. It was from those two experiences that Walt's Pilgrimage was born.

I had always wanted to visit Marceline, Missouri to see Walt's hometown and thought about gathering some fellow Disney fans for a road trip to Chicago (to see the birth home) and Marceline. I shared the idea with my dear friend and university colleague, Julia Primavera  Kuntz, who told me that my idea sounded like a "Study in the States" trip offered by Western Michigan University's Lee Honors College in Kalamazoo. So the fun road trip became an official college course. Then the course inspired this book. I wanted others in the world to experience the life of Walt Disney in this way.

This is an experiential way of learning Walt's story. While other Walt tours exist, they include just a small portion of what this travel guide includes. It is the most comprehensive guide to sites associated with the life of Walter Elias Disney, a man whom I have admired my entire life. I have been to more than 80 of these sites thus far and look forward to seeing them all! Enjoy walking in his footsteps throughout North America. Grab your mouse ears and hit the road!

-Christopher
aka "Mr. Pixie Dust"

Acknowledgements & Thank Yous

First, I would like to thank Dr. Carla Koretsky, former Dean of the WMU Lee Honors College, for making this Pilgrimage possible through the unique Study in the States Program. Dean Koretsky offered me the once-in-a-lifetime opportunity to lead the inaugural "Disney Pilgrimage" in July 2015 for 8 WMU students who were selected for the trip. And I am grateful that interim Dean Jane Baas and the new Dean, Dr. Gary Bischof, supported the continuation of this course.

Second, I would like to acknowledge my pilgrimage partner-in-crime, Julia Primavera Kuntz. "Jules" helped us successfully navigate the first pilgrimage involving nearly 25 hours of time in a 12-passenger van, two flights, and a crazy adventure up to Mineral King and back (pre-Rocco Kuntz). Jules was a god-send on the trip and was the one who encouraged me to take my personal idea of the  pilgrimage and transform it into an educational experience for college students. We will forever have this Walt Disney bond.

 Next, I would like to commend the 8 WMU students who had the honor of participating in the first Disney Pilgrimage: Christy Baumeister, Elizabeth Blasko, Erin Caspers, Nikki Finkler, Joshua Grimmer, Gabriel Vivan, Kurt Wendland, and Annalisa Wilder. Thank you for embarking on such an incredible journey of walking in Walt's footsteps!

A very special thank you to Dave Smith, Chief Archivist Emeritus of The Walt Disney Archives, who reviewed the book for accuracy and provided the necessary edits. His contribution is much appreciated.

Thank You to...

Anthony Helms and Monica de Los Santos who were a part of one or more of Walt's Pilgrimages. Anthony was our chauffeur through 3 states for 3 years (and counting)!

Nick Andreadis, Dean Emeritus of the WMU Lee Honors College, for originating the Study in the States Program. It is an amazing program that enables creative faculty minds to create engaging experiences and enables students to learn in a dynamic and interactive way.

Kevin Robert Ryan for designing the cover and the state, province, and country maps.

Chelsey Miller for designing the icons used throughout the chapters.

Maya Sheth for designing the Walt Passport Stamp.

Donna St. John for her valuable proofreading skills and suggested edits.

Sharon Carlson of the WMU Archives for confirming some information in the chapter about Walt's visit to Kalamazoo in 1964.

Kaye Malins who reviewed the Marceline chapter for accuracy and provided a testimonial.

Fred Colgren and his colleagues who reviewed the Gilmore Car Museum chapter for accuracy.

Sr. Dorothy K. Ederer, O.P., who introduced me to book publishing.

Dr. Jeff Barnes (aka "Dr. Disneyland") who reviewed the section on Disneyland and for providing a testimonial.

Mike and Linda Pohl for the field trip to The Henry Ford.

Greg Kaplan for his self-publishing suggestions.

Fareed Shalhout who took the Elias Disney Pilgrimage with me to finalize that content for the book.

Crag Bretz who accompanied me to SUNY Fredonia to photograph Disney Hall.

Caitlin Moneypenny-Johnston, Head of Brand Management and Permissions at The Walt Disney Family Museum, for reviewing that chapter.

Pat Cummings-Witter, Library Clerk for Archives and Special Collections of the Daniel A. Reed Library at SUNY-Fredonia who tracked down information about Disney Hall there.

Wendy Tackett for her thorough review and suggested edits. She was a God-send. We are forever connected through Disney and WMU!

Kevin McAlpine for informing me about the "Suitcase and a Dream" performance at Disney California Adventure.

The individuals who provided feedback and input about the final cover designs: Sr. Dorothy K. Ederer, O.P., Susan Sheth (and the GATE team), Stefanie Billue, Sheila and Richard Roe, Wendy Tackett, Kristin Gartner, Monica de Los Santos, Julia Primavera Kuntz and Jeff Barnes.

All of the Disney scholars, historians, researchers, and authors whose work I relied on to compile this Pilgrimage.

Ron Miller for writing the Foreword to the book. It has been my honor to meet you and interact with you during our annual visits to the Walt Disney Family Museum. Your generosity and support is appreciated.

Finally, I wish to thank all of the presenters and hosts who generously shared their time and talent on the annual pilgrimages over the years:

Chris and Dave Ankeney, Jeff Barnes, Michael Botkin, Becky Cline, Fred Colgren, Sarah Dunham, Alyson Fried, Patricia Gonzalez, Bob Gurr, Louise Jackson, Inez Johnson, Kirsten Komoroske, Cathy Lean, Kaye Malins, Doug Marsh, Ron Miller, Charlie Pipal, Todd Regan, Steve Sligh,

Jacob Smallegan, Dave Smith, Mary Beth Switzer, Kimi Thompson, Dan Viets, Michael Wells, Jon Wearley, Peter Whitehead, and Chris Wolff. I am humbled by your hospitality, knowledge, and engagement with Walt's Pilgrimage.

About the Student Contributors

Western Michigan University students from the 2016 university course (Pilgrimage 2.0) assisted with the compilation of elements for this book:

Carly Dauer
Katelyn Drummond
Emily Fackler
MacKayla Myszka
Megan Schaefer
Brendan Schneider
Kirsten Stowell
Hannah Truckenbrod

About Study in the States

 The Lee Honors College signature Study in the States program provides students with an innovative, hands-on, cultural experience and valuable learning opportunity. Students enrolled in these courses complete an intensive one to two week journey with a small group of their peers and an expert WMU faculty member. All expenses (except tuition) are paid by the honors college. Students earn honors credit and experience the United States in an entirely diverse and unique way (Courtesy of Renée Allen).

How to Use This Book

This book is a guide for all types of Walt Disney fanatics.

While designed as a travel guide, non-travelers and Disney history buffs will enjoy this sense of place in Walt's life. This book is part history, part adventure.

ENTIRE PILGRIMAGE

The entire Pilgrimage, which includes more than 275 stops in 84 cities in 25 states plus Canada and Mexico. If you do the entire Pilgrimage, please contact me as I would love to hear about your journey.

ORIGINAL WALT'S PILGRIMAGE

The original 8-day college course pilgrimage included stops in these 9 major cities/metropolitan areas: Chicago-Marceline-Kansas City-San Francisco-Mineral King-Valencia-Los Angeles-Anaheim-Burbank/Glendale.

SPEND A DAY IN A CITY

Perhaps you only have time to visit one city at a time. This book enables you to spend a day in a city exploring some or all of the places that hold a Disney connection.

These 4 cities have the largest number of sites to explore:

Kansas City, MO:	33 sites
Los Angeles, CA:	27 sites
Marceline, MO:	15 sites
Chicago, IL:	13 sites

SELECT PLACES THAT INTEREST YOU

As you learn about all of the potential destinations included in this book, you may choose places that interest you based on the aspects of Walt's life that matter to you – or destinations close to where you live.

SUGGESTED MINI ROUTES
Chicago-Marceline-Kansas City (Chapters 41, 53, 52)
Los Angeles Area (Chapters 2-7, 9, 17, 20, 21, 22, 24, 25)

DISNEY PARKS PILGRIMAGE
Anaheim: Disneyland (and Disney California Adventure)
Lake Buena Vista: Walt Disney World

ELEMENTARY SCHOOLS PILGRIMAGE
Visit all 15 elementary schools named after Walt Disney
in 10 states (see pages 341-342).

TREMBLAY'S "MUST SEE" SELECTIONS
 There are 21 "must see" sites in 9 cities:
Anaheim (CA), Glendale (CA), Los Angeles (CA),
San Francisco (CA), Mineral King (CA), Lake
Buena Vista (FL), Chicago (IL), Kansas City (MO), and
Marceline (MO). Look for the binoculars icon.

WALT'S PASSPORT
At the end of each chapter is "Walt's
Passport." Use the Passport to check
off the sites as you visit them. The
special passport stamp features
Walt's birthdate. The passport
watermark is Sleeping Beauty
Castle in Disneyland.

Sites and destinations in 21 primary states/district and 2 countries are covered
in this Pilgrimage: Alaska, California, Connecticut, Florida, Hawaii, Idaho, Illinois,
Iowa, Kansas, Louisiana, Massachusetts, Michigan, Missouri, New Jersey, New
York, Ohio, Oregon, Pennsylvania, Virginia, Washington, and Washington D.C.
plus Canada and Mexico. The states are listed in alphabetical order within this
book, which contains the major and minor sites in Walt's life. Canada and
Mexico follow the United States. Nearly 30 sites no longer have the original
structures. However, I have included them for the hard-core Disney fans who
wish to visit them.

15

ICONS AND LEGEND

For each site, icons will help inform you about the various aspects to consider:

	Admission Fee
	Drive-By Location
	Food Available
	Guided Tour Available
	Hotel Accommodations Available
	Multimedia
	Must See
	Not Open to the Public
	Original Structure Gone
	Parking Fee
	Post Death Tribute
	Site connected to Walt's love of Trains

Foreword by Ron Miller

Son-in-Law of Walt Disney
Husband of Diane Disney Miller
President, Board of Directors, Walt Disney Family Museum

Christopher & Ron in 2015

A few years ago, I was contacted by Christopher Tremblay about meeting his group of students from Western Michigan University during their visit to The Walt Disney Family Museum. Christopher explained that the students were taking a course on the life of Walt Disney, which culminated in a pilgrimage to the most influential places in Walt's life. The Walt Disney Family Museum in San Francisco, which was founded in 2009 by Walt's daughter and my late wife, Diane Disney Miller, was one of the stops along their journey.

I was impressed by Christopher's commitment and dedication to the subject of my father-in-law. People the world over know the Disney name, but not many people know much about the actual man behind one of the world's most recognized brands. Indeed, the desire to expose more people to the real story of Walt's life—a man from humble beginnings, who always stayed true to his vision and imagination, and who didn't let major setbacks and failures deter him from his dreams—was a major motivation behind Diane's drive to establish a living biography of her father.

The original concept was modest. But as Diane developed plans to implement her vision, she realized that, to properly honor her father, she had to create something truly spectacular—which she did in stunning fashion. The Walt Disney Family Museum opened in October 2009. The museum is a gorgeous, inspiring, expansive, state-of-the-art anchor institution in the iconic Presidio of San Francisco, a National Park that overlooks the Golden Gate Bridge.

Three years ago, and again this past year, I had the pleasure to meet Christopher and his astute and curious students when they visited the museum along their ambitious and enlightening trek. They asked interesting and thoughtful questions about Walt, including what his favorite color was. My answer: "He was Walt Disney—he liked every color."

I am grateful that Christopher has included the museum along his annual journey, as the museum is the quintessential place to discover Walt Disney, the man. I am also grateful to Christopher for helping impart the true story of Walt Disney—not only to teach students about Walt's great accomplishments, but also to inspire people to heed their imaginations and persevere in the face of adversity. This is the museum's mission, and it is what Diane wanted to pass along to future generations in honor of her father.

I am happy to have been part of this pilgrimage, and I thank Christopher for including the museum along the way. I hope that you are inspired by Christopher's book. And by Walt's story.

Ron Miller

To learn more about Ron, visit:
waltdisney.org/about/board-of-directors/ron-miller

Walt Disney's Family
An Overview

While there are more Disney family members included in this book, these individuals are mentioned most frequently:

Walter Elias Disney
Nickname: Diz

Lillian (Bounds) Disney
Wife of Walt Disney
(also known as Lilly)

Diane Marie (Disney) Miller
Daughter of Walt and Lillian Disney

Sharon Mae (Disney) Lund
Daughter of Walt and Lillian Disney

Roy O. Disney
One of Walt's older brothers who served as his business partner in the company

Edna Francis Disney
Wife of Roy O. Disney

Elias Disney
Father of Walt Disney

Flora (Call) Disney
Mother of Walt Disney

Disney Family Tree

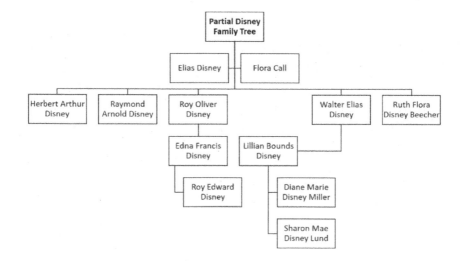

Walt Disney Recognition Day

United States of America

December 5, 1986
(Honoring Walt's Birthdate of December 5, 1901)

"The Congress, by Public Law 99-391, has designated December 5, 1986, as 'Walt Disney Recognition Day' and authorized and requested the President to issue a proclamation in observance of this event.

Now, Therefore, I, Ronald Reagan, President of the United States of America, do hereby proclaim December 5, 1986, as Walt Disney Recognition Day. I call upon all Americans to recognize this very special day in the spirit in which Walt Disney entertained young and older Americans" (Proclamation 5585 – Walt Disney Recognition Day, 1986, n.d., n.p.).

Walt Disney Days

September 24, 1955
Walt Disney Day
State of Pennsylvania

November 15, 1965
"Disney Day"
Dubbed by the Florida
Development Commission

December 15, 1967
Walt Disney Memorial Day
Marceline, Missouri

December 5, 1986
Walt Disney
Recognition Day
United States of America

December 5, 2013
Walt Disney Day
City of Chicago

October 16 (annually)
Walt Disney –
'A Day to Dream' Day
State of Missouri

ALASKA

W Candle

Food Available

Guided
Tour Available

Not Open to
the Public

Original Structure
Gone

Train
Connection

Parking
Fee

Post Death
Tribute

Hotel

Must See

Multimedia

Admission
Fee

Drive By
Location

Chapter 1
Candle, Alaska

Significance: In August 1947, Walt Disney and his daughter Sharon went to Candle, Alaska for a three-week trip at the invitation of friend/neighbor Russell Havenstrite, who was a gold mine owner and owned the town. Lillian Disney chose not to go because of how rough it can be up there, according to Diane Disney Miller (Thomas, 1994; WDFM, 2016).

Candle is located in the Northwest Arctic Borough, which had a 2010 population of about 7,500 people. The borough was formed on June 2, 1986 (Northwest Arctic Borough, 2017).

According to Diane Disney Miller:
"[Sharon and Dad] flew up over in this plane which is a DC3 Lincoln Bird. There was another couple along with them by the name of Anderson. In this one town they stayed in the airplane hangar and Daddy took care of my sister all the way" (WDFM, 2016, n.p.).

There is nothing Disney related to see here.

CALIFORNIA

Norden
Olympic Valley
Sacramento
Yosemite
San Francisco
Three Rivers/Mineral King
Santa Barbara
Palm Springs
Greater Los Angeles Area

Food Available

Guided Tour Available

Not Open to the Public

Original Structure Gone

Train Connection

Parking Fee

Post Death Tribute

Hotel

Must See

Multimedia

Admission Fee

Drive By Location

Chapter 2
Anaheim, California

Disneyland content consultant: Jeff Barnes (Dr. Disneyland)

Disneyland
1313 Disneyland Drive
Anaheim CA 92802
(714) 781-4565
disneyland.disney.go.com

Significance: Walt's first theme park and the only park he created that he ever walked in.

In August 1954, the first orange tree was removed to make room for Disneyland (Thomas, 1998).

Opened/Dedicated on July 17, 1955
Walt's last visit to Disneyland: October 14, 1966

"Disneyland would be a world of Americans, past and present, seen through the eyes of imagination – a place of warmth and nostalgia, of illusion and color and delight," stated Walt Disney (Smith, 1994, p. 29).

Anaheim, California was selected as the site for Disneyland based on the recommendation of the Stanford Research Institute, who conducted a survey commissioned by Walt (Smith, 2006).

Thomas (1998) refers to Disneyland's birthplace as the "rickety" bungalow that was moved from the Hyperion Studio to the Burbank studio.

 24 Must Sees:

Tunnel Plaques
"Here you leave today and enter the world of yesterday, tomorrow and fantasy." Written by Walt himself and installed two weeks after the park opened.

MAIN STREET, U.S.A.

Main Street, U.S.A.
Main Street, U.S.A. pays tribute to Walt's childhood of Marceline, Missouri. Walt's intention was to "present an idealized town at the turn of a century" (Smith, 2006, p. 424). Main Street, U.S.A. runs from the Disneyland Railroad Station to the Central Hub (2 blocks long) (Smith, 2006).

Disneyland Dedication Plaque and Walt's Dedication Speech

"To all who come to this happy place: Welcome. Disneyland is your land. Here, age relives fond memories of the past, and here youth may savor the challenge and promise of the future. Disneyland is dedicated to the ideals, the dreams, and the hard facts that have created America, with the hope

that it will be a source of joy and inspiration to all the world" (From photograph of the plaque).

 Watch Walt deliver the dedication speech of Disneyland. Search "Walt Disney's Opening Day Dedication Speech at Disneyland 1955" in YouTube.

 Disneyland Railroad
disneyland.disney.go.com/attractions/disneyland/disneyland-railroad

Walt was a train enthusiast. After building his own miniature railroad at his Carolwood Estate, he featured a railroad encircling Disneyland (and now at every Disney theme park around the world). This railroad is 1.2 miles long and features an 18-minute ride around the park. Ride the Disneyland Railroad to honor Walt's passion for trains.

 Disneyland Railroad Train Station
Photographs and memorabilia of Walt's love for trains appear in the train station (Strodder, 2015).

Disneyland Railroad:
Lilly Belle Train Car
    This train car is an "elegantly
furnished caboose on the Disneyland
Railroad formerly used for transporting
VIPs" (Smith, 2006). You typically cannot
ride in it and it is not always out/visible at
the park.

Lillian Disney was influential in designing
the car, adding family photos and
memorabilia. Because of her involvement, the car was named for
her (Doyle, 2014).

Opera House
The Opera House in Main Street, U.S.A. contains a large 3D
model of Disneyland as it was on opening day, a movie about
Walt, a park bench from Griffith Park and pays tribute to Walt's
interest in railroads (Disneyland Resort, 2017).

Windows Affiliated with Walt
Disneyland Casting Agency – 'It takes People to Make the Dream
a Reality' – Walter Elias Disney, Founder & Director Emeritus. It is
located above the Main Street Cinema and is dedicated to the
cast (personal communication, D. Smith, July 5, 2017).
An identical window is located in Walt Disney World's Magic
Kingdom Main Street, U.S.A.

There is also a tribute window for Christopher D. Miller,
Walt Disney's grandson (West Center Street).

There is also a tribute window honoring Elias Disney, Walt's
father (just above the Emporium).

Walt's Apartment

Above the fire station in Main Street, U.S.A. is Walt's apartment. The lamp in the window is always on to remind us that Walt's spirit is always in the park (except during the holiday season when the lamp is replaced by a Christmas tree). It is 500 square feet and was a place for Walt and his family to gather and spend time in private within Disneyland.

"A rose motif was used in the apartment extensively on everything from furniture to dinnerware, since it was a favorite of Walt's wife, Lillian, and in keeping with the time period" (Korkis, December 21, 2016, n.p.). According to Korkis (December 21, 2016), "Lillian's last known visit to the apartment was in December 1984" (n.p.).

Watch a video that tours the apartment and features Diane Disney Miller, Walt's daughter. Search "Inside Walt's Apartment With Diane Disney Miller | Disneyland Park" on YouTube.

Penny Arcade

Above the Penny Arcade is a giant penny dated 1901, the year Walt was born (Strodder, 2015).

Hotel Marceline

Located in Main Street, U.S.A., Hotel Marceline is a nod to Walt's hometown of Marceline, Missouri. It is just a façade. Chapter 53 (starts on page 257) is all about Marceline.

CENTRAL HUB

Original Partners Statue

Located in front of Sleeping Beauty Castle.

This bronze statue of Walt Disney with Mickey Mouse was installed in 1993, in honor of Mickey Mouse's 65th birthday. It was created by sculptor Blaine Gibson (Korkis, 2011).

"A former Disney animator and Imagineer, Blaine took one year to create the sculpture and based his depiction of Walt on a bust he originally created in the 1960s" (WESH2, December 10, 2014).

According to Gibson, "Walt was pointing down Main Street and saying to Mickey at his side, 'Look at all the happy people who have come to visit us today'" (Korkis, 2011).

In the statue, Walt is wearing a tie with the initials "STR" (for Smoke Tree Ranch) (WESH2, December 10, 2014). See pages 101-103 for more information about Smoke Tree Ranch.

(Note: The Partners Statue also appears in the Magic Kingdom at Walt Disney World, the Disney Legends Plaza, Tokyo Disneyland, and the Walt Disney Studios Park Paris) (personal communication, D. Smith, July 5, 2017).

Baby Care Center
This location features Walt's baby photo (Strodder, 2015).

First Aid Building
This location features a tribute window honoring Doc Sherwood, M.D., who bought one of Walt's early horse drawings in Marceline (Strodder, 2015).

ADVENTURELAND

Walt Disney's Enchanted Tiki Room

disneyland.disney.go.com/attractions/disneyland/enchanted-tiki-room/

"Enchanted Tiki Room—which debuted in 1963—is the first Audio-Animatronics show. Walt Disney's fascination with translating his love of film animation into the real world led to the groundbreaking new technology, which enabled the synchronization of movement, audio and visual effects of a multitude of animated figures at one time. This technology helped pave the way for other classic attractions, including 'It's a Small World,' 'Pirates of the Caribbean,' and the 'Haunted Mansion.' Walt originally envisioned Enchanted Tiki Room as a dinner show. However, he knew the attraction would be so popular that he changed the format to accommodate more guests before it opened" (Disneyland, n.d.b, n.p.).

FRONTIERLAND

The Golden Horseshoe

On July 13, 1955, Walt and Lillian Disney celebrated their 30th wedding anniversary with a "Tempus Fugit Celebration" in Disneyland at the Golden Horseshoe (Thomas, 1994, p. 270).

Petrified Tree

Walt gave this mineralized Petrified Tree to Lillian as an anniversary gift. Lillian donated it to Disneyland in 1957 (Strodder, 2015). It is located along the banks of the Rivers of America near The Golden Horseshoe.

"On July 11, 1956, Walt Disney purchased the remains of a petrified tree that once stood 200 feet tall from the Pike Forest Fossil Beds, a privately owned petrified forest area in Colorado that is now part of Florrisant Fossil Beds National Monument. Walt arranged for the tree to be sent to California" (Rivera, October 22, 2009).

Inscription of the Plaque:

PETRIFIED TREE
FROM THE
PIKE PETRIFIED FOREST, COLORADO
THIS SECTION WEIGHS FIVE TONS AND MEASURES 7 1/2 FEET
IN DIAMETER. THE ORIGINAL TREE, ESTIMATED TO HAVE
BEEN 200 FEET TALL, WAS PART OF A SUB-TROPICAL FOREST
55 TO 70 MILLION YEARS AGO IN WHAT IS NOW COLORADO.
SCIENTISTS BELIEVE IT TO BE OF THE REDWOOD OF SEQUOIA
SPECIES. DURING SOME PREHISTORIC ERA A CATACLYSMIC
UPHEAVAL CAUSED SILICA LADEN WATER TO OVERSPREAD
THE LIVING FOREST. WOOD CELLS WERE CHANGED DURING THE
COURSE OF TIME TO SANDSTONE. OPALS WERE FORMED
WITHIN THE TREE TRUNK ITSELF.

PRESENTED TO DISNEYLAND
BY
MRS. WALT DISNEY
SEPTEMBER, 1957

NEW ORLEANS SQUARE

Club 33

 Named after its location at 33 Royal Street. Private membership required. Opened June 15, 1967 (after Walt's death).

Significance: During Walt's work with the 1964-1965 World's Fair in New York (see pages 282-284), he noticed that corporations had VIP Lounges for guests, which gave him an idea to create a VIP Lounge, called Club 33, in Disneyland. Walt wanted a space for his corporate sponsors and other VIPs.

"In April 1966, Walt and Lillian Disney travelled to New Orleans with designer Emile Kuri, who had decorated the sets of *Mary Poppins* and *20,000 Leagues Under the Sea*, to select many of the beautiful antiques which would be featured in the club" (Glover, August 18, 2011).

21 Royal

(714) 300-7749
21royaldisneyland.com

Only available through private reservation.

Significance: This was once going to be a "private residence once envisioned by Walt and Lillian Disney as a secluded family retreat and a luxurious oasis in which to host celebrities and dignitaries" (21 Royal, n.d., n.p.).

Located above Royal Street in New Orleans Square (upstairs from Pirates of the Caribbean).

21 Royal can be booked for up to 12 guests. The $15,000 fee includes a seven-course meal (including dessert), park admission, valet service and tips (Strutner, January 27, 2017).

21 Royal was previously the Disneyland Dream Suite, which was a part of the "Year of a Million Dreams" promotion that ran from October 1, 2006 through December 31, 2008. In that dream suite, each room was themed after a distinct area of Disneyland. Prior to that (from July 1987 to August 2007), that space was known as the Disney Gallery.

Guests have the option of riding the Lilly Belle (see page 28) to 21 Royal (Baham, August 28, 2017).

FANTASYLAND

King Arthur Carrousel
A nod to Walt's time at the Griffith Park Merry-Go-Round (see pages 64-65). Walt insisted that all 72 horses had to leap.

Mr. Toad's Wild Ride
In the waiting area for this ride, there is a mural that features a train that has "WED RAIL" on it, a tribute to Walter Elias Disney (WED) (Strodder, 2015).

MICKEY'S TOONTOWN

Tribute Window
Above the library is a tribute window that reads "Laugh-O-gram Films, Inc." on top and "W.E. Disney, Directing Animator," a nod to Walt's business in Kansas City (Strodder, 2015). (For more information about Laugh-O-gram Films, see pages 242-243).

"Walk in Walt's Disneyland Footsteps" Guided Tour
disneyland.disney.go.com/events-tours/disneyland/walk-in-walts-disneyland-footsteps

Call (714) 781-8687 for reservations.
Not available every day of the week.
All ages permitted.
You may book a tour 30 days in advance.
Separate admission to Disneyland is required.
A three-and-a-half hour tour, inclusive of lunch.

"Depending on the time of day, end your historic tour with a delicious lunch or dinner on Main Street, U.S.A., provided for all tour participants by the Jolly Holiday Bakery"
(Disneyland, n.d.a, n.p.).

A collectible souvenir from this tour may also be available:

"The Walk in Walt's Disneyland Footsteps Tour pin is a coveted piece in any collection. Opening like a small book, this pin includes inspiration from Walt Disney" (Disneyland, n.d., n.p.).

Downtown Disney District

1580 Disneyland Drive
Anaheim CA 92802

Marceline's Confectionary

disneyland.disney.go.com/shops/downtown-disney-district/marcelines-confectionery/

 This sweets shop is another nod to Walt's Marceline, Missouri roots. Chapter 53 is all about Marceline.

Disney California Adventure

1313 Disneyland Drive
Anaheim CA 92802
(714) 781-4565
disneyland.disney.go.com/destinations/disney-california-adventure/

BUENA VISTA STREET

Storytellers Statue

 This is a bronze statue featuring Walt Disney and Mickey Mouse and was dedicated on June 15, 2012. It is a counterpart to the Partners Statue (see page 30). It is located in front of the Carthay Circle Theatre. This statue is designed to depict Walt as if he had just arrived in Los Angeles in 1923. Two plaques at the statue include a Walt Disney quotation "We are just getting started" and a comment referencing July 1923. This statue can also be found at Tokyo Disney Sea and Shanghai Disneyland in China (Storytellers (Statue), n.d.).

Red Car Trolley News Boys
These street performers pay tribute to Walt's 1923 journey to California on Buena Vista Street singing the original song "Suitcase and a Dream" (Red Car Trolley News Boys, 2017).

 Watch the performance on YouTube: https://www.youtube.com/watch?v=o6aBHcF7Tx4

1901

Significance: It honors the year Walt Disney was born, 1901.

 This is a private club located in Carthay Circle Theatre in Buena Vista Street. It is for Club 33 members only. It opened on June 15, 2012 (Glover, 2012).

"'Imagine it's the 1930s, and this is where the animators would've hung out, swapped stories, doodled on napkins," as 1901 is described by Imagineer Ray Spencer. 'This is the place Walt and the animators might've chatted, relaxed, unwound . . . a cozy den'" (Glover, 2012, n.p.).

"The lounge [is] decorated with personal artwork and photographs of the animators from the early years of the Walt Disney Studios, including some with Walt Disney's own signature. 'The guest is sort of an insider in this backstage world'" (Glover, 2012, n.p.).

Inside are two sets of Director's Chairs: One set for Walt and Lillian and another set for Roy O. and Edna Disney (This Fairytale Life, May 30, 2014).

Elias & Co.

disneyland.disney.go.com/shops/disney-california-adventure/elias-and-co/
A shop on Buena Vista Street.

Significance: Named after Walt's father, Elias Disney.

HOLLYWOOD LAND

Hyperion Theatre

Significance: Honors the Walt Disney Studio located on Hyperion, which operated from 1926 to 1940 at 2719 Hyperion (see page 74) (Smith, 2006).

A 2,000-seat theater in the Hollywood Pictures Backlot.

Walt Disney Elementary School

Magnolia School District
2323 West Orange Avenue
Anaheim CA 92804-3474
(714) 535-1183
magnoliasd.org/schools/walt-disney

Significance: An elementary school named in Walt's honor (1 of 15). (See pages 341-342 for the complete list of Walt Disney elementary schools).

On March 30, 1957, the school was dedicated. "Without notice to teachers, parents, or faculty, Walt declared a school holiday and invited the entire student body to Disneyland as his personal guests" (Disney Avenue, 2016, n.p.).

ANAHEIM

- ☐ Disneyland
- ☐ Disney California Adventure
- ☐ Downtown Disney
- ☐ Walk in Walt's Footsteps Tour
- ☐ Walt Disney Elementary School

ARRIVED
5 DEC 1901
WALT DISNEY

WALT'S PASSPORT

Chapter 3
Burbank, California

Walt Disney Studios
500 South Buena Vista Street
Burbank CA 91521
(818) 560-1000
waltdisneystudios.com

Significance: Walt built this studio which opened in 1940.

In June 1938, Walt and Roy put a $10,000 deposit down on 51 acres for this new studio. The move was complete by May 1940 (Korkis, 2015).

Originally, the Studio used 2400 West Alameda as its address. Buena Vista Street inspired the name of the Buena Vista Distribution Company (Smith, 2006).

This studios "campus" is home to 21 buildings/sites:

Team Disney:	Stages 6 & 7
Michael D. Eisner Building	Hyperion Bungalow
Disney Legends Plaza	Main Theater
Frank G. Wells Building	Ink and Paint Building
Animation Building	Cutting Building
Water Tower	Shorts Building
Roy O. Disney Building	Roy E. Disney Animation Building
Annette Funicello Stage (Stage 1)	ABC Studios Building
Julie Andrews Stage (Stage 2)	Digital Studios Center
Stage 3	Original Commissary
Stages 4 & 5	

The commissary once had an executive dining room called the Coral Room (Thomas, 1998). According to Thomas (1998), Walt's table was the first one on the right where he dined with celebrities and reporters.

Walt's Office
Walt's Office was "3H" wing on the third floor of the Animation Building (Korkis, 2015). In December 2015, Walt's office was restored to its original state as it was on the day of his death. Several Disney family members [including 3 granddaughters: Michelle Lund (Sharon's daughter), Joanna Miller (Diane's daughter), and Jennifer Goff (Diane's daughter)] were present for the dedication of the office. Walt's Office is only accessible to Disney employees, cast members, and D23-eligible members (D23, 2015).

"The five-room office suite includes a secretary's office with a cabinet holding Disney's many awards — such as a reproduction of the special Oscar he won for *Snow White and the Seven Dwarfs* with a normal-sized statuette and seven smaller ones — as well as Walt's working office, his formal office and a private area where he relaxed after a long day's work. In the formal office, Disney would host large meetings with his staff and visitors. It features items from his miniatures collection and photos of his daughters, as well as their bronzed baby shoes and Norman Rockwell drawings of them behind his desk. In the opposite corner is a piano where composers would play their scores for upcoming films when pitching them" (Garland, 2015, n.p.).

In late 1941, the studios became the home to 500 soldiers, becoming what Thomas (1998) referred to as a "war plant" (p. 151). The studios produced war films and designed 1,400 insignias for the military units (Thomas, 1998).

Get a sneak peek inside Walt's Office. Search "Walt Disney's restored office suite tour at Walt Disney Studios lot" on YouTube.

For more information, visit:
d23.com/walt-disneys-office-suite-restored-as-permanent-exhibit-space/

"Disney Art School"
Walt established the "Disney Art School" at the Disney studio. Don Graham, a teacher from Chouinard (see pages 76-77), taught classes two nights a week on the soundstage (B. Thomas, 1994). The first class was held on November 15, 1932 and 25 artists attended.

Walt Disney Archives
Frank G. Wells Building
Walt Disney Studios
500 S. Buena Vista Street
Burbank CA 91521-3040
(818) 560-5424
disney.archives@disney.com
d23.com/walt-disney-archives

Significance: A collection of historical materials related to Walt and the company he founded.

Not open to the public. However, "Qualified writers and other members of the public working on special projects can make advance appointments by special permission" (The Walt Disney Company, n.d., n.p.).

The Walt Disney Archives is located within the Walt Disney Studios.

"It seems to me that we have a lot of story yet to tell."
–Walt Disney (From the Walt Disney Archives brochure)

The Walt Disney Archives was established in 1970. Its first Director was Dave Smith. The Archives has more than 9,000 boxes of documents and merchandise, four million photographs, and several thousand historical props and costume pieces (The Walt Disney Company, n.d.).

The Archives is located in the building that honors the former President of The Walt Disney Company from 1984–1994, Frank G. Wells. The building opened in 1998 and was dedicated by Wells' widow, Luanne Wells, and then company CEO Michael Eisner.

Becky Cline is the current Director of the Walt Disney Archives, serving in that role since 2010.

About Dave Smith

Dave Smith joined the company on June 22, 1970, as its first archivist. His first task was to document all the items in Walt Disney's office which had sat dormant since Walt's death in 1966. In 1969, Dave wrote the first Disney bibliography. Dave retired from The Walt Disney Company in 2010 with 40 years of service. Dave has published numerous Disney books. In 2007, he was honored with the Disney Legends Award (D23, n.d.).
For more information, visit:
d23.com/walt-disney-legend/dave-smith/.

Disney Legends Plaza

Located next to the Team Disney Building within
The Walt Disney Studios.

Significance: The Disney Legends honor the spirit of Walt.

This plaza was
dedicated on October
16, 1998, in honor of
the 75th anniversary of The Walt Disney Company
(D23 Disney Fan Club, n.d.c).

"The Legends are chosen by a selection committee, formerly
appointed and chaired by the late Roy E. Disney. Since its
inception, the program has honored many gifted animators,
Imagineers, songwriters, actors, and business leaders as having
made a significant impact on the Disney legacy. The Plaza
features a second edition of the bronze sculpture first placed in
Disneyland Paris, with bronze plaques representing the
individual Legends lining the columns of the Plaza"
(D23 Disney Fan club, n.d.c, n.p.).

"The Disney Legends award has three distinct elements that characterize the contributions made by each talented recipient:

- The Spiral—stands for imagination, the power of an idea.
- The Hand—holds the gifts of skill, discipline and craftsmanship.
- The Wand and the Star—represent magic: the spark that is ignited when imagination and skill combine to create a new dream" (D23 Disney Fan Club, n.d.c, n.p.).

Induction into Disney Legends was annual at first and now it is every two years and coincides with the annual D23 Expo (Great Ideas Creative Group, 2015).

The Disney Legends Awards began in 1987 (Smith, 2006).

Disney Family Member Inductees

Class of 1998 Inductee: Roy E. Disney (Walt's nephew)
Class of 2003 Inductee: Edna F. Disney (Walt's sister-in-law)
Class of 2003 Inductee: Lillian Disney (Walt's wife)

Partners Statue

This statue of Walt Disney with Mickey Mouse was installed in 1999. It was created by sculptor Blaine Gibson (Korkis, 2011). The original Partners Statue is at Disneyland. Other copies of this statue are in the Magic Kingdom at Walt Disney World, Tokyo Disneyland, and the Walt Disney Studios Park in Paris (personal communication, D. Smith, July 5, 2017). For more information about the Partners statue, see page 30.

St. Joseph's Hospital

(now Providence St. Joseph Medical Center)
501 South Buena Vista Street
Burbank CA 91505
(818) 843-5111
providence.org/saint-joseph

Significance: Where Walt Disney died on December 15, 1966.

Walt had been hospitalized since November 30, 1966. He celebrated his 65th birthday in the hospital on December 5 (Thomas, 1994).

The hospital is located right across the street from The Walt Disney Studios.

Inside is a life-size statue of Roy and Edna Disney, created by Andrea Favilli, an Italian sculptor (Madden, 2017).

Virtual Tour
california.providence.org/saint-joseph/news/2012/05/the-roy-and-patricia-disney-family-cancer-center-virtual-tour/

Burbank was also the city to hold the first classes for the California Institute of the Arts (CalArts), before the campus in Valencia, California was ready (See Chapter 24).

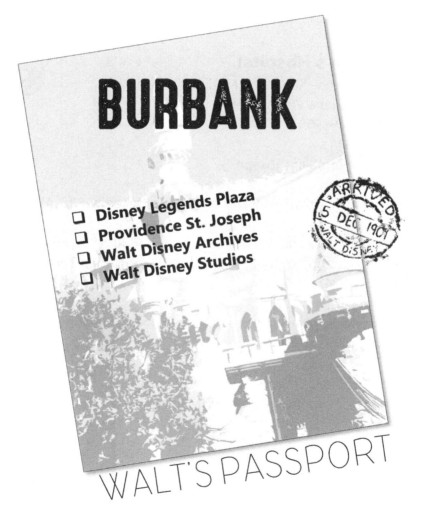

BURBANK

☐ Disney Legends Plaza
☐ Providence St. Joseph
☐ Walt Disney Archives
☐ Walt Disney Studios

ARRIVED
5 DEC 1901
WALT DISNEY

WALT'S PASSPORT

Chapter 4
Garden Grove, California

"Disney Garage Studio"
Garden Grove Historical Society's
     Stanley Ranch Museum
     and Historical Village
12174 Euclid Street
Garden Grove CA 92842
(714) 530-8871
ci.garden-grove.ca.us/HistoricalSociety/disney

 No admission fee, but donations are accepted.

Significance: The garage where Walt built the stand for his animation camera in 1923. It was originally located at 4406 Kingswell Avenue, Los Angeles, CA (home of Walt's Uncle, Robert – see page 59).

 Public tours are available the first and third Sunday of each month at 1:30 p.m. Special tours during the week for 8 or more can be arranged.

"The garage, originally owned by Robert Disney (uncle of Roy and Walt Disney) in North Hollywood, was used by Walt as a studio when he came to California in 1923. It was saved from demolition in 1984 by The Friends of Walt Disney, who housed, insured, and generously donated the historical building to the Stanley Ranch Museum" (City of Garden Grove, n.d., n.p.).

To learn more, read:
Walt Disney's Garage of Dreams by Arthur C. "Buddy" Adler.
Available from Theme Park Press.

GARDEN GROVE

ARRIVED
5 DEC 1901
WALT DISNEY

☐ **Disney Garage Studio**

WALT'S PASSPORT

Chapter 5
Glendale, California

Compilation of information assisted by Hannah Truckenbrod

Walt Disney Imagineering™ (WDI)

1401 Flower Street
Glendale CA 91201
disneyimaginations.com/about-imaginations/about-imagineering
wdi.disneycareers.com

Significance: Walt Disney Imagineering (WDI) was formed by Walt originally as WED Enterprises (based on Walt's initials). It officially opened on December 16, 1952. It was established to develop plans for Disneyland and to manage Walt's personal assets. Originally an independent, private company owned by Walt himself, it was merged into Walt Disney Productions in 1965. It is better known today for designing and building the world famous Disney Parks and resorts all across the globe.

Imagineering = Imagination + Engineering

"We're always exploring and experimenting. At WED, we call it Imagineering – the blending of creative imagination with technical know-how," stated Walt Disney (Smith, 1994, p. 28).

Walt set up a secret room at WDI for the Florida Project (aka Walt Disney World) (Watts, 1997).

"Walt Disney Imagineering (WDI) is the creative force that imagines, designs and builds all Disney theme parks, resorts, attractions and cruise ships worldwide. Imagineering's unique strength comes from its diverse global team of creative and technical professionals, who build on Disney's legacy of storytelling to pioneer new forms of entertainment"
(The Walt Disney Company, 2017, p. 1).

Over 125,000 pieces of original art are in the archives of Walt Disney Imagineering. This includes the original 1953 concept sketch of Disneyland (The Walt Disney Company, 2017).

In 1963, WDI created the first Audio-Animatronics figures for Walt Disney's Enchanted Tiki Room at Disneyland
(The Walt Disney Company, 2017) (See page 31 for more information).

As of 2017, there were 1,700 imagineers employed with Walt Disney Imagineering. Walt Disney Imagineering holds more than 100 U.S. patents (The Walt Disney Company, 2017).

"Well, WED is, you might call it my backyard laboratory, my workshop away from work," stated Walt Disney
(Smith, 1994, p. 96).

Watch a 2-minute Video about Walt Disney Imagineering, featuring Walt's voice in the beginning:

disneyimaginations.com/about-imaginations/about-imagineering/

Forest Lawn Cemetery

1712 South Glendale Avenue
Glendale CA 91205
(323) 254-3131
forestlawn.com/glendale

Significance: Burial site of Walt Disney's cremated ashes and other Disney relatives.

Walt Disney died at 9:30 a.m. on December 15, 1966, the result of an acute circulatory collapse (Thomas, 1994).

Also buried in this cemetery are Walt's parents (Elias and Flora) and Walt's brother, Raymond Arnold Disney.

Walt Disney's gravesite is located near the Freedom Mausoleum. Also buried with him is Robert B. Brown (Sharon's first husband), and Lillian Bounds Disney (Walt's wife). Noted on the plaque is Walt's daughter, Sharon Disney Brown Lund. She is not buried there; her ashes were scattered in Hawaii (personal communication, D. Smith, July 5, 2017).

Walt's private funeral service was held at the Little Church of the Flowers (according to Dave Smith). Only Walt's immediate family was present for a simple service on December 16, 1966, the day after he died (Thomas, 1994). In lieu of flowers, the family asked that donations be made to the California Institute of the Arts (CalArts) (see Chapter 24) (Thomas, 1994). Roy Edward and Patty Disney provided a wreath (Thomas, 1998).

Walt once said, "When I'm dead, I don't want a funeral, I want people to remember me alive" (Miller, 1956, p. 114).

Roy O. Disney issued this official statement about Walt's death: "Walt built an organization with the creative talents to carry on as he had established and directed it through the years. Today this organization has been built and we will carry out this wish" (Watts, 1997, p. 447).

There is a great tribute to the world's reaction of Walt's death in an exhibit at The Walt Disney Family Museum (See Chapter 19).

Other Disney Relatives
Elias and Flora Disney (Walt's parents) are buried in the Great Mausoleum, in the Sanctuary of Truth (Space 5493 for Flora; Space 5499 for Elias). The Sanctuary of Truth is not open to the public; only members of the Disney family.

Flora Call Disney died on November 6, 1938. Elias Disney died on September 13, 1941. For more information about Walt's parents, see Chapter 74.

Sharon Disney Brown Lund died on February 16, 1993.
Lillian Bounds Disney (Walt's wife) died on December 16, 1997.

Raymond Arnold Disney is located in the Sanctuary of Prayer within the Freedom Mausoleum. Space 20400. Raymond died on May 24, 1989. Raymond was in the insurance business (Smith, 2006).

A map of Forest Lawn Glendale can be found online here:
cemeteryguide.com/ForestLawn-Glendale3D.jpg

 Download the Forest Lawn Visitors Guide app:
forestlawn.com/app/
(However, Walt Disney is not listed).

Southern Pacific Railroad Depot

Now the Glendale Transportation Center
400 West Cerritos Avenue
Glendale CA 91204
(800) 872-7245
glendaleca.gov/government/departments/community-development/urban-design-mobility/glendale-transportation-center

Significance: "As an adult, it gave him (Walt) great pleasure to visit the Southern Pacific station in Glendale a few miles from his Los Feliz Home, to feel the vibrations of the tracks, and then watch the passenger trains pass through on the route to San Francisco" (Thomas, 1994, p. 213).

This Center is now an Amtrak and Metrolink rail station.

GLENDALE

☐ **Forest Lawn Cemetery**
☐ **Glendale Transportation Center**
☐ **Walt Disney Imagineering**

ARRIVED
5 DEC 1901
WALT DISNE

WALT'S PASSPORT

Chapter 6
Hollywood, California

Hollywood Walk of Fame

Hollywood Boulevard
Hollywood CA 90028
(323) 469-8311
walkoffame.com/walt-disney

Significance: Tributes to Walt Disney and his career in animation and television. Both of Walt Disney's stars were installed on February 8, 1960.

Star of Motion Pictures
7021 Hollywood Boulevard
Hollywood CA 90028

Star of Television
6747 Hollywood Boulevard
Hollywood CA 90028

"The Hollywood Walk of Fame is a historical landmark located in Hollywood, California which consists of five-pointed terrazzo and brass stars embedded in the sidewalks along fifteen blocks of Hollywood Boulevard and three blocks of Vine Street" (Disney Wiki, n.d.a, n.p.).

"The Hollywood Walk of Fame is an internationally-recognized Hollywood icon. The man credited with the idea for creating a Walk of Fame, was E. M. Stuart, who served in 1953 as the volunteer president of the Hollywood Chamber of Commerce. In that year, according to a Chamber press release, he proposed the Walk as a means to 'maintain the glory of a community whose name means glamour and excitement in the four corners of the world'" (HWOF, n.d., n.p.).

In addition, to Walt, Roy O. Disney has a star, along with Disneyland, Mickey Mouse, Donald Duck, Snow White, Tinker Bell, and Winnie the Pooh (Disney Wiki, n.d.).

The Walk of Fame runs 1.3 miles east to west on Hollywood Boulevard from Gower Street to La Brea Avenue.

Hollywood Athletic Club

6525 Sunset Boulevard
Los Angeles CA 90028
(323) 460-6360
thehollywoodathleticclub.com

Significance: In 1931-1932, Walt went there 2-3 times a week for boxing calisthenics and swimming (Thomas, 1994). Lillian also swam at the club and both did horseback riding.

Walt Disney is referenced in the history on the club's website.

Hollywood Brown Derby

1628 North Vine Street
Hollywood CA 90028

Significance: Walt and Lillian would often dine here.

According to Jim Korkis (2015), there is a historical marker just outside that address that shares the story of the Derby.

HOLLYWOOD

- ☐ Walt's Star of Motion Pictures
- ☐ Walt's Star of Television
- ☐ Hollywood Athletic Club
- ☐ Hollywood Brown Derby

ARRIVED
5 DEC. 1901
WALT DISNEY

WALT'S PASSPORT

Chapter 7
Los Angeles, California

27 sites to explore

Compilation of information assisted by Megan Schaefer

Walt's Uncle's Home: Robert Disney

(Charlotte and Robert Disney House)
4406 Kingswell Avenue
Los Angeles CA 90027
laconservancy.org/locations/charlotte-and-robert-disney-house

Walt lived here from July 1923 to Fall 1923.

Significance: Walt's first residence in Los Angeles in 1923.
He paid $5/week in rent.

The freestanding garage at Robert
Disney's home was used by Walt
upon arriving in Los Angeles (This
garage is now located in Garden
Grove. See Chapter 4 for more
information.).

"This one-story craftsman bungalow is significant as the first
home of Walt Disney in Los Angeles and the location of his first
local animation work. The house was owned by Disney's Uncle
Robert and Aunt Charlotte, and 21-year-old Walt relocated to
Los Angeles in 1923 and began his animation work in the garage
while boarding with them at this residence" (Los Angeles
Conservancy, 2016, n.p.). This house was built in 1914, according
to the Los Angeles Conservancy.

In 2016, this home was about to be demolished. However, papers were filed and the house has been designated a Historical-Cultural Monument (Los Angeles Conservancy, 2017).

 Silent Home Movies in front of the house featuring Walt Disney: Search "Walt Disney: Family Home Movies" on YouTube.

Rooming House: Room Walt Shared with Roy

4409 Kingswell Avenue
Los Angeles CA 90027

Walt lived here from 1923 to 1925.

Significance: Walt's second residence in Los Angeles.

Walt and Roy lived across the street from Uncle Robert Disney (Thomas, 1994).

Walt and Lillian's First Apartment

4637 North Melbourne Avenue
Los Angeles CA 90027

Significance: Walt's third residence in Los Angeles. Walt and Lillian lived here from August 1925 to December 1925 (Thomas, 1994).

Walt and Lillian's Second Apartment

1307 North Commonwealth
Los Angeles CA 90027

Walt and Lillian lived here from to December 1925 to December 1927.

Significance: Walt and Lillian's second home together (Thomas, 1994).

Walt and Lillian's First Home

2495 Lyric Avenue
Los Angeles CA 90027

Walt and Lillian lived here from December 1927 to Fall 1933.

Significance: Walt and Lillian's first home. They paid about $7,000 (Thomas, 1994).

"The houses were built from modified prefabricated kits manufactured by the Pacific Ready Cut Homes Company. Michael Barrier noted in his book, *The Animated Man*, construction on the two homes began in August of 1926 and was completed by the following December. The cost of the land and the two kit houses was estimated by Roy Disney to be approximately $16,000" (2719 Hyperion, June 29, 2015, n.p.; Barrier, 2007).

Tam O'Shanter Restaurant

2980 Los Feliz Boulevard
Los Angeles CA 90039
(323) 664-0228
lawrysonline.com/tam-oshanter

Significance: Walt was a frequent diner at the "Tam," eating at Table 31.

 The Tam opened in 1922 and serves pub fare with a Scottish touch. It is known for its prime rib and Yorkshire pudding.

According to Jim Korkis (2015), the Tam O'Shanter opened as the Montgomery Inn and renamed the Tam O'Shanter in 1925, becoming a Scottish Inn. Walt and his staff came to the Tam O'Shanter for lunch because the Disney studio did not have a commissary (Korkis, 2015).

Walt's Barn

Located at Los Angeles Live Steamers Museum
Griffith Park
5202 Zoo Drive
Los Angeles CA 90027
carolwood.com/walts-barn
carolwood.org/barn.html
(818) 934-0173
combine@carolwood.org

Significance: This is the actual barn that Walt had at his Holmby Hills home. Walt had a huge love for railroads.

Admission and Parking are Free

The Barn is open on the third Sunday of each month from 11 a.m. to 3 p.m. Donations to the Los Angeles Live Steamers Museum are accepted.

This barn was rededicated on July 19, 1999: "In memory of Walt Disney and his love for railroading he shared with the world." Diane Disney Miller (Walt's daughter) was present for this event.

"Walt Disney's Barn Museum, the original Santa Fe & Disneyland Combine Coach, and Ollie Johnston's Victorian Train Depot, are open for public visiting. Informative volunteer Barn Crew members are on hand to describe the history and contents. Often, Disney veterans and Legends drop by for chats and autographs" (Carolwood, n.d.a, n.p.).

"When the Holmby Hills home was sold, the new owners had plans to preserve the house, but discovered that due to structural issues and asbestos, they demolished the existing structures and built a new home. Fortunately, Walt's daughter Diane Disney Miller recognized the importance of the Barn and began the process of saving it before escrow closed. Diane contacted Michael and Sharon Broggie, founders of the Carolwood Society, who began planning what to do with the Barn. A general contractor, Bill Abel, was hired to dismantle the Barn and it was stored until an agreement was secured with the City of Los Angeles and the Los Angeles Live Steamers Museum. It opened in Griffith Park as a loan to the people of Los Angeles on July 19, 1999, and is located inside the 1/8th scale track, the same scale that Walt had at his home" (Carolwood, n.d.b, n.p.).

Griffith Park Merry-Go-Round

4730 Crystal Springs Drive
Los Angeles CA 90027
(323) 665-3051
laparks.org/griffithpark/griffith-park-merry-go-round

Open weekends throughout the year and weekdays during the summer, and over Christmas and Easter vacations, 11 a.m. to 5 p.m.

Be sure to ride the Merry Go Round!

Significance: Walt would bring his daughters, Diane and Sharon, to ride the merry-go-round at Griffith Park. Part of this location inspired Disneyland.

There is a plaque on a bench that reads:

"The actual park bench from the Griffith Park Merry-Go-Round where Walt Disney first dreamed of Disneyland."

Another bench next to the Merry-Go-Round reads: "Walt, Diane, and Sharon: They Loved this Carousel."

"Located in Park Center between the Los Angeles Zoo and the Los Feliz park entrance, the Griffith Park Merry-Go-Round has been a Los Angeles family attraction for over five generations. Built in 1926 by the Spillman Engineering Company and brought to Griffith Park in 1937, the Merry-Go-Round boasts 68 horses, everyone a jumper. Each horse is finely carved with jewel-encrusted bridles, detailed draped blankets and decorated with sunflowers and lion's heads. A Stinson 165 Military Band Organ, reputed to be the largest band organ accompanying a carousel

64

on the West Coast, plays over 1500 selections of marches and waltz music" (Los Angeles Department of Recreation and Parks, n.d., n.p.).

"According to Walt Disney, the idea for a Disney-themed amusement park came to him while sitting on a park bench. He thought about creating a new kind of amusement park, while he watched his daughters ride the Griffith Park Merry-Go-Round" (Findingmickey.com, n.d., n.p.).

Walt Disney Concert Hall (WDCH)

111 South Grand Avenue
Los Angeles CA 90012
(323) 850-2000
laphil.com/visit

Opened on October 24, 2003 (took 16 years to create and build)
Home to the Los Angeles Philharmonic

Significance: Named in honor of Walt Disney at the request of Lillian Disney and her $50 million donation.

Tours Available (guided and self-guided):
musiccenter.org/support/Give-Now/Exploring-the-Center/

"Lillian B. Disney, in honor of her late husband Walt Disney, donated $50 million to the Music Center for a new concert hall. The Disney family had a long-standing association with the Music Center, and the donation was a reflection of her husband's love of music, a love he had shared with the world in his collaboration with conductor Leopold Stokowski to combine classical music with animation in the 1940 film *Fantasia*" (Walt Disney Concert Hall 10th Anniversary, 2013, n.p.).

"First and foremost, the concert hall...must be designed and built...to be one of the finest in the world and serve as a permanent tribute to my late husband, Walt Disney," stated Lillian Disney (Walt Disney Concert Hall 10th Anniversary, 2013, n.p.).

"Designed by architect Frank Gehry, Walt Disney Concert Hall (WDCH) is an internationally recognized architectural landmark and one of the most acoustically sophisticated concert halls in the world. From the stainless steel curves of its striking exterior to the state-of-the-art acoustics of the hardwood-paneled main auditorium, the 3.6-acre complex embodies the unique energy and creative spirit of the city of Los Angeles and its orchestra. Thanks to the vision and generosity of Lillian Disney, the Disney family, and many other individual and corporate donors, Los Angeles enjoys the music of the Los Angeles Philharmonic, the Los Angeles Master Chorale and visiting artists and orchestras from around the world" (The Los Angeles Philharmonic, 2017, n.p.).

Spaces/Plaques Connected to Walt Disney

Outside Brick: Diane Disney Miller's name appears

Donor Wall--Cornerstone Donors:
- Lillian B. Disney
- The Walt Disney Company
- Diane and Ron Miller
- The Sharon Disney Lund Foundation
- Patricia and Roy Edward Disney

Second Donor Wall: The Walt and Lilly Disney Foundation*

*

The Walt and Lilly Disney Foundation
(formerly The Lillian B. Disney Foundation)
P.O. Box 2566
San Anselmo CA 94979-2566

Established in 1974 by Lillian Disney.
San Anselmo is just north of San Francisco.

The President of the Foundation is Walter Elias Disney Miller (Walt's grandson), the Secretary/Treasurer is Ron Miller (Walt's son-in-law) and the Vice President is Christopher D. Miller (Walt's grandson).

Blue Ribbon Garden
The Concert Hall's rooftop garden.

"A Rose for Lilly" – Frank Gehry's tribute to Lillian Disney as a
gift of her grandchildren and great-grandchildren.

"Nearly an acre in size, the garden is tucked beneath the hall's gleaming exterior and filled with lush landscaping that blooms throughout the year. One of the garden's highlights is *A Rose for Lilly*, the Frank Gehry-designed fountain that pays tribute to the late Lillian Disney and her love for Royal Delft porcelain vases and roses. The fountain is a large rose that's covered in thousands of broken pieces of Delft porcelain and tiles, creating a one-of-a-kind mosaic. The Blue Ribbon Garden often serves as a backdrop to pre- and post-theater receptions, private events and children's programming"
(Discover Los Angeles, 2017, n.p.).

On the street, wrapped around a pole across from the concert hall, is the history about Walt Disney Concert Hall, including a photo of Lillian Disney.

TIP: Be sure to pick up the "Architectural and Garden Highlights" brochure.

Disney Affiliated:

REDCAT
631 West Second Street
Los Angeles CA 90012
(213) 237-2800
redcat.org

Significance: Dedicated to Walt's brother and sister-in-law: Roy O. and Edna Disney. It opened in November 2003 as a part of The Walt Disney Concert Hall.

"The Roy and Edna Disney/CalArts Theater (REDCAT) is an interdisciplinary contemporary arts center for innovative visual, performing and media arts located in downtown Los Angeles inside the Walt Disney Concert Hall complex. Each season REDCAT presents a far-reaching roster of work by globally renowned artists, inside one of the most versatile and technologically advanced presentation spaces in the world" (REDCAT, 2016, n.p.).

For more information about CalArts, see Chapter 24.

DuBrock's Riding Academy

(now home to L.A. Shares)
3224 Riverside Drive
Los Angeles CA 90027

Significance: Walt, Roy, and six others from the studio staged their polo practices here. Their actual matches took place at the Riviera Country Club in Pacific Palisades (See Chapter 15).

Walt's Los Feliz Home

4053 Woking Way
Los Angeles CA 90027

Significance: Home where Walt lived from 1932 to 1950.

"In 1932 Walt and Lillian had their Los Feliz home built at 4053 Woking Way, Los Angeles, CA. This is where they raised their children and became a family. The Disneys lived here from 1932 until 1950 when they moved to their Carolwood home" (Findingwalt.com, n.d., n.p.).

Facts about this House:

- "Walt Disney designed the home with architect Frank Crowhurst, who worked on a tower addition to the Hyperion Studio.

- The $50,000 12-room home combines elements of Tudor and French Normandy styles and includes four bedrooms, four-and-a-half baths, a screening room, a gym room with sleeping porch, and a pool and pool house, among other details.

- The house was built in two months and was constructed by a crew largely composed of out-of-work, Depression-era workers.

- The building was rushed in order to be ready for the birth of Walt and Lillian's first child, but she tragically miscarried. They went on to have Diane in 1933, and adopt Sharon in 1936.

- The family would gather in the screening room to watch movies and dailies from the studio" (Radish, 2014, n.p.).

Walt Disney's Carolwood Estate

Holmby Hills Neighborhood
355 North Carolwood Drive
Los Angeles CA 90077

Significance: On June 1, 1948, Walt and Lillian bought the lot for this new house. Walt built a home here and moved in February, 1950. Walt lived there until he died in 1966. Lillian remained living there until her death in 1997. It was a 3.7 acre estate.

"In the new estate's backyard Walt Disney built a one-eighth-scale steam railroad, inspired by the ones his company's animators (Ward Kimball and Ollie Johnston) had implemented on their own properties. He erected a standalone barn housing a control room and carved out a half-mile worth of track including overpasses, a 46-foot-long trestle and an s-shaped subterranean tunnel hidden underneath his wife's flower beds. The train would famously come to be known as the Carolwood Pacific Railroad and it would serve as part of the inspiration to create Disneyland, the first of his eponymous theme parks" (Brennan, 2013, n.p.).

Walt included a soda fountain for his two daughters (Watts, 1997).

The original house was razed and a new mansion was built on the site in 2001 by Gabriel Brener, according to Brennan (2013).

While Walt's home is not there, the 90-foot underground tunnel is still there. "Its entrance is marked by an ivy-covered miniature stone archway with the date "1950" – the year the railroad began operating – etched on it" (Brennan, 2013).

The barn and track are now located at the Los Angeles Live Steamers in Griffith Park (see pages 64-65).

The Walt Disney Family Museum displayed a 3D model of this home in 2016-2017 as part of a "Home for the Holidays" special exhibit (WDFM, n.d.).

ABOUT HOLMBY HILLS
"Holmby Hills is an affluent neighborhood in the district of Westwood in western Los Angeles. It is bordered by the city of Beverly Hills on the east, Wilshire Boulevard on the south, Beverly Glen Boulevard on the west, and Bel Air on the north.

Sunset Boulevard is the area's principal thoroughfare which divides Holmby Hills into north and south sections" (Holmby Hills, Los Angeles, n.d., n.p.).

Disney Brothers Cartoon Studio

4651 Kingswell Avenue (and 4649)
Los Angeles CA 90027

Significance: Site of the very first working Disney studio in Los Angeles.

"Both [Walt and Roy] of us were unemployed and neither could get a job. We solved the problem by going into business for ourselves. We established the first animated cartoon studio in Hollywood," stated Walt Disney (D23 Disney Fan Club, n.d.b, n.p.).

"The Walt Disney Company started in 1923 in the rear of a small office occupied by Holly-Vermont Realty in Los Angeles. It was there that Walt Disney, and his brother Roy, produced a series of short live-action/ animated films collectively called the Alice Comedies. The rent was a mere $10 a month. Within four months, the ever-growing staff moved next door to larger facilities, where the sign on the window read 'Disney Bros. Studio'" (Walt Disney Studios, n.d., n.p.).

"The studio became too small for their growing number of employees – they boasted a staff of seven by February [1924] – and so Walt and Roy decided to expand the space by renting the adjacent store at 4649 Kingswell" (Madden, 2017, p. 51).

Hyperion Studio

Now the Site of Gelson's Market
2719 Hyperion Avenue
Los Angeles CA 90027

Significance: Walt's next commercial studio space from 1926 to 1940. Site of the Animation School for the Walt Disney Studios from 1935 to 1940.

In 1925, Walt and Roy placed a $400 down payment on this land. Roy had selected this location. The Disney brothers spent $3,000 to renovate the existing building there (Korkis, 2015).

"It was this studio that Disney produced the last of the Alice Comedies, all of the Oswald the Lucky Rabbit shorts, and the early Mickey Mouse and Silly Symphony shorts" (Korkis, 2015, p. 11).

The roof of this building had a neon sign that indicated this was the home of Mickey Mouse. Additions were put on, including a sound stage and animator's building (Korkis, 2015).

There is a "Point of Historical Interest" sign acknowledging the site of Walt Disney's original animation studio in Los Angeles. It is on Hyperion Avenue in front of the parking lot.

According to Korkis (2015), "The Hyperion location was declared a historical-cultural monument in October 6, 1976 and marker No. 163 was installed" (p. 13).

Carthay Circle Theatre

6316 San Vicente Boulevard
Los Angeles CA 90035

Significance: On December 21, 1937, *Snow White and the Seven Dwarfs* premiered to a record-breaking audience at this theatre.

"Originally built in 1926, The Carthay Circle Theatre stood out among its neighboring structures thanks to its beautiful architecture. The single-screen theatre played home to many different theatrical performances including silent movies, live magic shows, and eventually feature films. The final performance of the Carthay Circle Theatre took place in November of 1968. The following year in 1969, the building was demolished due to a variety of reasons. On the property now stands several office buildings, and a small park dedicated to the historic theater" (Young, 2009).

About the Disney – Carthay Circle Theatre Connection:
"News clippings from the time quote theatre manager Ray Ducerne, who reported that advance ticket sales outpaced every other picture ever booked at the theatre, resulting in a sold-out opening night. Advance demand for tickets was so strong that sales were limited to four per person. More than 30,000 fans who couldn't score one of the $5 tickets gathered outside the theatre just to be a part of the historic event" (Glover, 2011, n.p.).

Vacant Lot (at the time)

4589 Hollywood Boulevard
Los Angeles CA 90027

Significance: "Walt rented a vacant lot at this intersection where he photographed live action with Virginia Davis and the neighborhood kids for his next film, *Alice Hunting in Africa*" (Thomas, 1994, p. 73).

Chouinard Art Institute

743 South Grand View Street
Los Angeles CA 90057
laconservancy.org/locations/chouinard-la-new-times-western-school

Now home to the LA New Times Western School, a Montessori preschool.

Significance: "In 1931, Walt arranged with Chouinard Art Institute in Los Angeles for his artists to attend night classes, with the studio paying the tuition" (Thomas, 1994, p. 115-116). Walt would drive his artists to and from school since they could not afford cars (Thomas, 1994). Thomas (1994) also noted that the "Chouinard Art Institute had given Disney artists free classes when the studio could not afford to pay for them" (p. 329).

Founded in 1921 by Nelbert M. Chouinard, the school was located in the Westlake section of Los Angeles, just south of MacArthur Park (CalArts, n.d.a).

In the late 1950s, Walt Disney provided money to help the school during challenging times (B. Thomas, 1994). However, "Walt realized that Chouinard's problems required more than periodic infusions of cash. He worked with his staff on ways to modernize the school, proposing a widened curriculum and a showcase where students could display and sell their art" (Thomas, 1994, p. 329).

"Walt Disney commissioned Economics Research Associates to survey the problems of Chouinard Art Institute and offer possible solutions" (Thomas, 1994, p. 330).

Chouinard Art Institute would merge with the Los Angeles Conservatory of Music to become the California Institute of the Arts (CalArts), proposed by Mrs. Lulu Von Hagen, the wife of a Los Angeles lawyer and businessman (Thomas, 1994). Chouinard operated on Grand View Street until 1970, when the CalArts campus opened (CalArts, n.d.a).

In 1956, Walt received an honorary degree from Chouinard Art Institute (Smith, 1994).

To see the list of Chouinard alumni: calarts.edu/about/institute/history/chouinard-art-institute

---

Marlborough School

250 South Rossmore Avenue
Los Angeles CA 90004
(323) 935-1147
marlborough.org

Significance: The school that Diane Disney (Walt's daughter) attended.

"Each weekday morning (Walt) made a wide circuit, delivering Diane to Marlborough School in the Wilshire District..." (Thomas, 1994, p. 197). Marlborough School is an independent college-preparatory secondary school for grades 7 through 12. This school opened in 1889 as St. Margaret's School for Girls (Marlborough School, n.d.).

Pan-Pacific Auditorium

(now the site of Pan-Pacific Park Recreation Center)
7600 West Beverly Boulevard
Los Angeles CA 90036
(323) 939-8874
laparks.org/reccenter/pan-pacific

Significance: In 1952, Walt exhibited a "miniatures" model of Granny's Cabin at a Festival of California Living here. Collecting miniatures was one of Walt's hobbies (Smith, 2016).

The original structure was destroyed in a fire. The entrance to Disney California Adventure is modeled after the Pan-Pacific Auditorium (personal communication, D. Smith, July 5, 2017).

Westlake School for Girls
(now Harvard-Westlake School)

Westwood
700 North Faring Road
Los Angeles CA 90007
(818) 980-6692
hw.com

Significance: The school that Sharon Disney (Walt's daughter) attended.

"Each weekday morning (Walt) made a wide circuit...taking Sharon to Westlake School in Westwood before going on to the studio in Burbank" (Thomas, 1994, p. 197).

Harvard-Westlake School is an independent, co-educational university preparatory day school consisting of two campuses located in Los Angeles, California, with approximately 1,600 students enrolled in grades seven through twelve (Harvard-Westlake School, n.d.).

"In 1904, Jessica Smith Vance and Frederica de Laguna opened the doors of Westlake School for Girls on Sixth Street and Alvarado Street, named for its location near Westlake Park in Los Angeles, now known as MacArthur Park. Westlake moved to a larger site on Westmoreland Avenue in 1917. In 1927, Miss Vance and Miss de Laguna acquired the land at the North Faring Road location from Harold Janss who wanted the School to become an anchor for the development of Holmby Hills" (Harvard Westlake, 2017, n.p.).

Gilmore Stadium

7899 Beverly Boulevard
Los Angeles CA 90036

Significance: Walt watched the Hollywood Stars baseball team at Gilmore Stadium (Thomas, 1994).

According to Diane Disney Miller, Walt and Lillian had a box at Gilmore Field in the 1940s and 1950s (Korkis, 2015). According to Korkis (2015), "The box was right behind the Stars' dugout, between first base and home plate. They (Walt and Lillian) attended most of the home games..." (p. 23).

It was opened in May 1934 and demolished in 1952. The stadium was located west of Curson Avenue, surrounded by Beverly Boulevard, Fairfax Avenue and Third Street. This site is now home to CBS Television City (Gilmore Stadium, n.d.).

Hollywood Bowl

2301 Highland Avenue
Los Angeles CA 90068
(323) 850-2000
hollywoodbowl.com

Significance: "On warm summer evenings, he (Walt) and Lilly listened to the Symphonies Under the Stars" here (Thomas, 1994, p. 226).

Check out the Hollywood Bowl Museum:
hollywoodbowl.com/visit/hollywood-bowl-museum

A self-guided tour is available:
hollywoodbowl.com/visit/hollywood-bowl-museum/museum#bowl-walk

---

Herbert A. Disney's Home

1915 Hollyvista Avenue
Los Angeles CA 90027

Significance: Home of Walt's brother, Herbert (Walt Disney Hometown Museum photograph).

Herbert was the oldest brother of Walt and was a mailman (Smith, 2006); his wife was Louise and he had a daughter, Dorothy (Burnes, Butler & Viets, 2002). He was born in Daytona Beach, Florida.

University of Southern California

Los Angeles CA 90089
(213) 740-2311
usc.edu

Significance: On June 4, 1938, Walt received his first (of three) honorary degrees, a Master of Science degree from the University of Southern California (D23 Disney Fan Club, n.d.d).

"USC President Rufus B. von KleinSmid, in bestowing the degree, praised Walt for 'bringing to youngsters the spirit of innocent childhood, and bringing to oldsters a bit of their second childhood'" (Barrier, 2015, n.p.).

Sawtelle Veterans Home

(Now the Veterans Affairs (VA) West Los Angeles Medical Center)
11301 Wilshire Boulevard
Los Angeles CA 90073
(310) 478-3711
losangeles.va.gov

Significance: Shortly after arriving in Los Angeles in 1923, Walt visited his brother Roy Disney at the Sawtelle Veterans Home, where Roy was recovering from tuberculosis (Mosley, 1992).

Pacific Finance Building

(Now the site of The Aon Center)
Corner of Wilshire Boulevard & South Hope St.
Los Angeles CA 90017

Significance: In the summer of 1953, Walt and Roy went to the Stanford Research Institute (SRI) office in this building to review 10 possible sites for Disneyland.

When you're in the Los Angeles area, dine at The Bel-Air Roadhouse, which is owned by Susan Disney Lord, a great niece of Walt Disney (granddaughter of Roy O. Disney):

The Bel-Air
662 North Sepulveda Boulevard
Los Angeles CA 90049

(310) 440 5544
thebel-air.com

LOS ANGELES

- ☐ Carthay Circle Theatre
- ☐ Chouinard Art Institute
- ☐ Disney Brothers Cartoon Studio
- ☐ DuBrock's Riding Academy
- ☐ Gilmore Stadium
- ☐ Griffith Park Merry-Go-Round
- ☐ Harvard-Westlake School
- ☐ Herbert A. Disney's Home
- ☐ Hollywood Bowl
- ☐ Marlborough School
- ☐ Pacific Finance Building
- ☐ Pan-Pacific Auditorium
- ☐ REDCAT
- ☐ Sawtelle Veterans Home

WALT'S PASSPORT

LOS ANGELES

- ☐ Tam O'Shanter
- ☐ Uncle Robert's House
- ☐ University of Southern California
- ☐ Vacant Lot
- ☐ Walt and Lillian's First Apartment
- ☐ Walt and Lillian's First Home
- ☐ Walt and Lillian's Second Apartment
- ☐ Walt Disney Concert Hall
- ☐ Walt Disney's Carolwood Estate
- ☐ Walt's Barn
- ☐ Walt's House on Woking Way
- ☐ Walt's Hyperion Studio
- ☐ Walt's Los Feliz Home

ARRIVED
5 DEC 1901
WALT DISN-

WALT'S PASSPORT

Chapter 8
Monte Rio, California

Bohemian Grove

20601 Bohemian Avenue
Monte Rio CA 95462

Located 75 miles north of downtown San Francisco.

Significance: Where Walt attended the Bohemian Club's retreat in July 1936 (see pages 113-114 for more information about the Bohemian Club).

This place is a 2700-acre campground belonging to the Bohemian Club. Every mid July, they host a two-week gathering of the world's most prominent men (Bohemian Grove, n.d.).

Only active members of the club and their guests may visit the Grove (Bohemian Grove, n.d.).

MONTE RIO

☐ **Bohemian Grove**

ARRIVED
5 DEC 1901
WALT DISNE

WALT'S PASSPORT

Chapter 9
Newhall, California

Golden Oak Ranch
19802 Placerita Canyon Road
Newhall CA 91321
(661) 259-8717
goldenoakranch.com

Significance: A 708-acre ranch Walt purchased on March 11, 1959 to use as a film location (Smith, 2006).

"Walt Disney first leased The Golden Oak Ranch in the late 1950s for the Spin and Marty segments of *The Mickey Mouse Club*. Because of the variety of natural settings available there, the Studio purchased the property in 1959 and, over the years, acquired additional land which has brought the total to just under 900 acres. Disney productions that have shot at the Ranch include: *Old Yeller, Toby Tyler, The Parent Trap, The Shaggy Dog, Follow Me Boys,* and more recently, *The Santa Clause, Pearl Harbor, Princess Diaries II* and *Pirates of the Caribbean II & III*" (Golden Oak Ranch, n.d., n.p.).

"Over the years, other motion picture and television production groups began filming at the Ranch and added to the variety of sets already there. A western street was created for the 1978 renowned television miniseries Roots II and remained active until its removal in 2008. Other sets and locations include a rural covered bridge on a lake, wood bridges, the Golden Oak Hall from the movie *The Country Bears,* farm houses, barns, fields, country roads, tree groves, a forest area, a creek bed, and our newest addition, Pine Lake, which includes a waterfall and was designed to give the feeling of a High Sierra setting" (Golden Oak Ranch, n.d., n.p.).

Places in Golden Oak Ranch have been featured in *Mame, Roots, The Waltons, Back to the Future, Dynasty* and *Little House on the Prairie* (Smith, 2006).

Note: Newhall, California and Valencia, California are nearby so you should check out both cities together. (See Chapter 24: Valencia).

Chapter 10
Norco, California
Nicknamed "Horsetown U.S.A."

Walt's Field Day at Lake Narconian Resort
Norco/Corona CA 92860

Significance: Walt threw a party for the success of
Snow White and the Seven Dwarfs here. Fourteen hundred
people attended.

The Narconian Resort Supreme is a former hotel/resort in Norco
(Corona), California, built in the 1920s, largely intact after over 70
years as a naval base and prison. Originally called the 'Lake
Norconian Club,' it opened on February 2, 1929"
(The Norconian Resort Supreme, n.d., n.p.).

"On the weekend of June 4, 1938, Walt rewarded his hard-
working staff with a 2-day party at the Lake Narconian resort
hotel near Palm Springs. It was a thank-you to the overworked
artists (their families were invited, too), who had worked scads of
unpaid overtime to turn out this milestone of a film before
Christmas, 1937" (Babbitt, 2012, n.p.).

"The Norconian Resort, built during the financial boom of the
1920s, featured a golf course, riding stables, a lake and marina, a
massive outdoor pool with diving platforms, a ballroom, and
luxury hotel accommodations. The facility, as described in a 1938
newspaper article, was proving itself a celebrity hot spot, popular
'among the members of the Hollywood movie colony.' In ways,
Walt was likely attracted to the Norconian because of its
reputation at other studios" (Pierce, 2013, n.p.).

Watts (1997) referred to this event as "perhaps the most famous
incident of studio debauchery" (p. 176).

Disney Legend Bill Justice said this about the event:
"Walt was horrified at the shenanigans. He and his wife drove home that next morning. He never referred to that party again and in fact if you wanted to keep your job, you didn't mention it either when you were working at the studio. We never had a party like that again" (Korkis, February 16, 2011, n.p.).

For a full account of this event, visit:
disneyhistoryinstitute.com/2013/09/walts-field-day-1938.html

 To listen to a podcast about Disney's Field Day:
DHI 003 – Walt's Field Day
itunes.apple.com/us/podcast/disney-history-institute-podcast/

Chapter 11
Norden, California

Compilation of information assisted by MacKayla Myszka

Sugar Bowl Resort & Mt. Disney

629 Sugar Bowl Road
Norden CA 95724
(530) 426-9000
sugarbowl.com

Hans Schroll, an avid skier in the 1930s, laid eyes on Mount Lincoln in California and immediately wanted to build lifts and runs up and down it. He used all of his money to seek out investors for his new ski resort. The Sugar Bowl Resort officially opened to the public in December 1939 (WDFM, 2012).

Now, the resort has various terrain and four distinct mountain peaks, short lines, uncrowded slopes, a lot of backcountry, and expert instruction for beginners to professionals.

Significance: One of Hans Schroll's first investors was Walt Disney. They became close friends when Walt was vacationing. Walt donated $2,500 and thus became one of the initial stockholders of the ski company. Schroll changed the name of one of the mountain peaks to Mount Disney (which stands at 7,953 foot elevation), in honor of his friend. After investing, Disney even vacationed at Sugar Bowl Resort with his wife Lillian and daughter Diane in 1941. Walt also sponsored events such as the Disney Junior Challenge Trophy and the Sugar Bowl Perpetual Goofy Races for children (WDFM, 2012).

To see the map with the reference to Mt. Disney and other uses of the Disney name: sugarbowl.com/stats

Disney References at Sugar Bowl Resort:
Disney Express (chairlift)
Disney Meadow (ski run)
Disney Nose (ski run)
Disney Return
Disney Traverse
Donald Duck (ski run)

NORDEN

☐ **Sugar Bowl Resort**
☐ **Mt. Disney**

ARRIVED
5 DEC 1901
WALT DISNEY

WALT'S PASSPORT

Chapter 12
North Hollywood, California

Television Academy Hall of Fame

5220 Lankershim Boulevard
North Hollywood CA 91601
(818) 754-2800
emmys.com/bios/walt-disney

Significance: Walt Disney was inducted into the Television Academy Hall of Fame in 1986.

Lillian Disney accepted the award on behalf of Walt.

The Hall of Fame is located in the outdoor Academy Plaza, in front of the new Academy of Television Arts & Sciences building in North Hollywood. This is an outdoor courtyard open to the public.

Walt's bust is located toward the back in front of the "Hall of Fame" sign. He is just left of Carol Burnett.

During Walt's lifetime, he and his Studio received 7 Emmy Awards (Smith, 2006).

ARRIVED
5 DEC. 1901
WALT DISNEY

NORTH HOLLYWOOD

☐ **Television Academy Hall of Fame**

WALT'S PASSPORT

Chapter 13
Oakland, California

Information was compiled with assistance by MacKayla Myszka

Children's Fairyland
Storybook Theme Park
699 Bellevue Avenue
Oakland CA 94610
(510) 452-2259
fairyland.org

Significance: Children's Fairyland is said to be one of the many inspirations for Disneyland. Walt incorporated ideas from Fairyland into Fantasyland. He even hired Fairyland's first executive director (Dorothy Manes) and one of its puppeteers.

Fairyland features sets from the storybook stories of *Alice in Wonderland* and *Peter Pan*, and they were built before the Disney films.

Fairyland opened in 1950 and was the brainchild of businessman Arthur Navlet and the Oakland Lake Merritt Breakfast Club, who raised $50,000 to build the park on the shores of Lake Merritt. The park featured themed storybook 'sets' with guides in costume who led the children through the landscape. There are gardens and original paintings that still reside in the park today. It is also home to the oldest continuously operating puppet theater in the United States (Children's Fairyland, 2016).

In the theme park, there are close to 60 storybook sets, kid-size rides, friendly animals, and 10 acres of gardens. Some of the sets include The Old Lady in the Shoe, Jack and Jill Hill, Peter Rabbit's Garden, The Jolly Roger Pirate Ship, and many more. The park is not filled with thrill rides, but rather attractions that encourage imagination and play. They do have a carousel, a mini ferris wheel, and a trolley. Animals are another important part of Fairyland's dynamic. They have domestic animals such as ponies, donkeys, rabbits, goats, sheep, ducks, guinea pigs, and chickens (Children's Fairyland, 2016).

OAKLAND

☐ **Children's Fairyland**

ARRIVED
5 DEC 1961
WALT DISNEY

WALT'S PASSPORT

Chapter 14
Olympic Valley, California

Site of the 1960 Winter Olympics

Squaw Valley Alpine Meadows Ski Resort
1960 Squaw Valley Road
Olympic Valley CA 96146
(800) 403-0206
squawalpine.com

Significance: Walt served as the chairman of the Pageantry Committee for the 1960 Winter Olympics in Squaw Valley.

"In 1958, Organizing Committee President Prentis Hale visited the Disney studio in Burbank and, after joining Walt for lunch, asked him to become Chairman of the Pageantry Committee for the upcoming Games" (WDFM, January 18, 2012, n.p.).

In the summer of 1959, Walt made several visits to the site as part of the planning (WDFM, January 18, 2012).

Walt "was responsible for producing both the opening and closing ceremonies. He organized an opening ceremony that included 5,000 entertainers, the release of 2,000 pigeons, and a military gun salute of eight shots, one for each of the previous Winter Olympic Games" (1960 Winter Olympics, 2017, n.p.).

Walt had a vacation home here during the time of his work with the Olympics; however, the location is unknown (Smith, 2012).

To read more, visit:
waltdisney.com/blog/new-heights-walt-and-winter-olympics

OLYMPIC VALLEY

☐ **Squaw Valley Ski Resort**

ARRIVED
5 DEC 1901
WALT DISNEY

WALT'S PASSPORT

Chapter 15
Pacific Palisades, California

The Riviera Country Club
1250 Capri Drive
Pacific Palisades CA 90272
(310) 454-6591
therivieracountryclub.com

Significance: Roy and Walt Disney played polo here. "Roy and Walt found themselves competing with Spencer Tracy, Leslie Howard, Darryl Zanuck, Jack Holt, Frank Borzage, and Will Rogers" (Thomas, 1998, p. 85). They played polo from 1933-1938 (Thomas, 1998). "Walt had played in matches that resulted in two fatalities...the end came when Walt took a spill and crushed four of his cervical vertebrae. A chiropractor manipulated Walt's back badly, leaving him with lifelong pain" (Thomas, 1998, p. 86).

PACIFIC PALISADES

☐ **Riviera Country Club**

ARRIVED
5 DEC 1901
WALT DISNE

WALT'S PASSPORT

Chapter 16
Palm Springs, California

Smoke Tree Ranch

850 Smoke Tree Lane
Palm Springs CA 92264-1602
(760) 327-1221
smoketreeranch.com

Significance: Walt owned a second home here (on two occasions). Walt also had a tie with the initials "STR" on it – for Smoke Tree Ranch.

One of Walt's vacation homes was located at 2688 S. Camino Real. Walt first visited Palm Springs in 1936 (Arthur, January 5, 2006).

According to Diane Disney Miller (Walt's daughter):
"My parents discovered Palm Springs in the late 1930s. We stayed at the B-H Guest House, and really loved it. It was all about the western theme: cowboys, horses, riding out across the desert to beautiful palm-studded canyons with streams that came down from the mountains. Somehow they heard about Smoke Tree Ranch, and that became the favorite destination. Smoke Tree had a 'colony' of home owners, and after many years staying in the very comfortable, appealingly simple guest cabins, my parents bought property there and built a home" (Walt Disney Family Museum plaque).

"Disney first came to the desert in 1936, to ride horses, to play polo and to camp out like the cowboys he admired...he was later responsible for creating the bowling green. Disney loved lawn bowling and even entered the tournaments held at the Ranch" (Palm Springs Homes and Condos for Sale, July 12, 2010, n.p.).

Walt and Lillian "established a Walt and Lilly Disney trophy for the annual bowling tournament that attracts bowlers from all over Southern California" (Crawford, 2010).

"That was when Charlie Doyle owned the ranch, and Disney reminisces, 'I remember Doyle trying to get me interested as a partner. I didn't have the money he thought I did, for I was still having problems financing my productions. Actually, it wasn't until after Mickey Mouse that we could afford to have a house there'" (Crawford, 2010, n.p.).

Walt became a member of Smoke Tree Ranch in 1946 and built his own house on the property in 1948 (D23 Disney Fan Club, n.d.e).

"The Disneys spent Easter, Thanksgiving and between Christmas and New Year's at Smoke Tree Ranch, a Palm Springs development where families maintained vacation houses, taking meals in a communal dining room" (Thomas, 1976, p. 226).

In 1954, Walt sold his Smoke Tree Ranch home to help build Disneyland. "Specifically, the money Walt raised through the sale of the home he had built in 1948 went to pay for two locomotives and the railroad track surrounding the Park (owned personally by Walt through WED Enterprises)" (Brock, n.d., n.p.).

In 1957, Walt bought a different home in Smoke Tree Ranch (D23 Disney Fan Club, n.d.e).

Walt's last visit to Smoke Tree Ranch was in November 1966 after Thanksgiving:

"Walt thought he might feel better if he went to the desert, and he and Lilly flew to Palm Springs. But he stayed only one night at the house at Smoke Tree Ranch. He grew weaker, and he returned to St. Joseph's Hospital on November 30" (Thomas, 1976, p. 353). Walt died 15 days later.

Walt Disney Hall
Smoke Tree Ranch's social hall is named for Walt Disney. It was built in the 1950s. It is available to rent for up to 120 people. smoketreeranch.com/meetingfacilities.html

One of Walt's neighbors was Donald Gilmore of Kalamazoo, MI. (see pages 219-220 for more information about the Gilmore Car Museum).

 Stay the night at one of the 49 cottages available for rent: smoketreeranch.com/cottages1.html

---

Palm Springs Municipal Airport
(now called Palm Springs International Airport)
3400 East Tahquitz Canyon Way
Palm Springs CA 92262
(760) 318-3800
palmspringsca.gov/government/departments/aviation-palm-springs-international-airport-psp

Significance: The airport Walt and Lillian would fly in/out of to get to Smoke Tree Ranch.

"Walt arranged to have the Disney Company Gulfstream airplane pick up Mr. and Mrs. [Donald] Gilmore, along with Walt and Lillian, at the Palm Springs airport on Monday April 4, 1966 at 9:30 a.m. to fly to Burbank to check the mocked-up, oversized interior [of *The Gnome-Mobile* set piece] at the Disney Studio. Walt had lunch with the Gilmores and then the Gulfstream flew them back to Palm Springs around 2 p.m. It was roughly a half-hour flight each way" (Korkis, May 11, 2016, n.p.).

PALM SPRINGS

- ☐ Smoke Tree Ranch
- ☐ Disney Hall
- ☐ Palm Springs International Airport

ARRIVED
5 DEC 1961
WALT DISNE

WALT'S PASSPORT

Chapter 17
Pasadena, California

Constance Hotel

(now the dusitD2 Hotel Constance Pasadena)
928 East Colorado Boulevard
Pasadena CA 91106
(626) 898-7900
dusit.com/dusitd2/pasadena/

Significance: Where Walt and his family viewed the Pasadena Rose Parade from a balcony on January 2, 1939. That was Walt's first visit to the Rose Parade (Walt Disney Family Museum photo caption).

Other Rose Parade connections:
In 1938, there was a *Snow White and the Seven Dwarfs* float in the parade (Smith, 2006).

In 1966, Walt served as the Grand Marshal in the parade (Smith, 2006).

PASADENA

☐ **Constance Hotel**

5 DEC 190? · ARKIVED · WALT DISNE

WALT'S PASSPORT

Chapter 18
Sacramento, California

California Hall of Fame

1020 O Street
Sacramento CA 95814
(916) 653-7524
californiamuseum.org

Significance: Walt Disney was a member of the first class of inductees in 2006. Diane Disney Miller (Walt's daughter) accepted the honor on his behalf. Frank Gehry (see Walt Disney Concert Hall on pages 65-69) read Walt's induction.

Because the exhibit changes annually, the panel honoring Walt Disney has not been on display since 2006. Therefore, there is nothing of Walt Disney to see here.

"The California Hall of Fame was established in 2006 by the Museum and former First Lady Maria Shriver to honor legendary people who embody California's innovative spirit and have made their mark on history. Inductees come from all walks of life and have made distinguished achievements across a variety fields, including the arts, education, business and labor, science, sports, philanthropy and public service"
(California Hall of Fame, 2017, n.p.).

For more information:
californiamuseum.org/inductee/walt-disney

 Watch the 2006 induction ceremony video:
californiamuseum.org/post/1st-annual-california-hall-fame

(Frank Gehry's introduction of Walt Disney begins at 30:50.)

SACRAMENTO

❑ **California Hall of Fame**

ARRIVED
15 DEC 1961
WALT DISNEY

WALT'S PASSPORT

Chapter 19
San Francisco, California

Information was compiled with assistance by MacKayla Myszka

(If you are traveling to the San Francisco area, be sure to check out Silverado Vineyards because of the Disney family connection – more information is on page 348).

The Walt Disney Family Museum

The Presidio
104 Montgomery Street
San Francisco CA 94129
(415) 345-6800
waltdisney.org

Open daily except for Tuesdays, January 1, Thanksgiving, and Christmas.

Significance: A museum dedicated to Walt's life, created by his daughter, Diane Disney Miller.

The Museum was founded in 2009 and is located in the Presidio of San Francisco, in former U.S. Army barracks renovated to fit the Museum's needs. The project was financed by the Walt Disney Family Foundation and the sale of bonds. It was created because the family, particularly Walt's daughter Diane, was tired of the unflattering biographies representing Walt. According to her, "They [The Walt Disney Company] try, but there is nobody there anymore who actually knew him" (Barnes, 2009, n.p.). "Disney the man, she frets, has gotten lost as his empire pushes its brand across the globe," stated *New York Times* author Brooks Barnes (2009, n.p.).

The Museum had the goal of focusing on the man instead of The Walt Disney Company brand and legacy. The museum sheds a better light on Walt, debunking myths about him in the process.

The Museum is located in San Francisco, instead of Los Angeles, because, at the time, most of the Disney family resided in Northern California. Diane wanted it to be closer to the family and did not want it to be associated with The Walt Disney Company (personal communication, D. Smith, July 5, 2017).

The main Museum building was "constructed in 1897 as Barracks 104 and was part of a row of massive, brick Army barracks on Montgomery Street that were built to house soldiers" (The Walt Disney Family Museum, 2017, n.p.).

The Walt Disney Family Museum follows the life of Walt from his birth in Chicago until the worldwide sadness of his death. In between are thousands of artifacts and stories regarding his lasting legacy on the world of entertainment. The museum is 40,000 square feet of interactive galleries featuring historic materials, early animations and drawings, movies, music, state-of-the-art technologies, audio stations, more than 200 video screens, and a spectacular model of Disneyland. There is even a small theater that shows Disney classics. The galleries featured are Early Beginnings, The Move to Hollywood, Exploring New Horizons, The Transition into Features, New Success & Greater Ambitions, Patriotic Contributions, Postwar Rebuilding, Walt & the Natural World, Disneyland & Beyond, and Remembering Walt Disney.

The Museum also presents numerous events, such as talks and workshops featuring Disney Legends (see pages 43-44), actors, animators, musicians, character voices, illustrators, stop-motion cinematographers, and voice-actors. Throughout the year, the Museum offers classes to encourage students of all ages to explore acting, special effects, animation, illusions, outdoor cinematography, and comic book heroes.

Diane Disney Miller Exhibition Hall
This space was dedicated and named for Walt's daughter, Diane, in March 2014. It houses the museum's rotating exhibitions and is located in a separate building at 122 Riley Avenue. Separate admission for special exhibits in this hall is typically required.

Most of the year, there are new special exhibitions that are showcased for limited times. *Wish Upon a Star: The Art of Pinocchio, Disney and Dali: Architects of the Imagination, Magic, Color, Flair: The World of Mary Blair, Awaking Beauty: The Art of Eyvind Earle*, and *All Aboard: A Celebration of Walt's Trains* are a few that the Museum has showcased.

 youtube.com/user/WDFMuseum

Fairmont Hotel

950 Mason Street
San Francisco CA 94108
(415) 772-5000
fairmont.com/san-francisco

Significance: "On December 19, 1941, a presentation of *The Art of Skiing* [a Disney movie featuring Goofy] was held at the Fairmont Hotel in nearby San Francisco as part of the California Ski Association's first annual Skiers Ball. Walt and Lillian attended the event and introduced the cartoon" (WDFM, 2012, n.p.).

Playland

Next to Ocean Beach
Across the street from:
  798 Great Highway
  San Francisco CA 94121

Significance: Walt Disney visited Playland a year before Disneyland opened. It was another inspiration for the happiest place on Earth. He also personally recruited George K. Whitney to be director of ride operations at Disneyland (Playland (San Francisco), 2016).

Playland was a seaside amusement park next to Ocean Beach. It started out as single oceanside attractions accessed by steam engine, starting in 1884, and then by trolley in 1890. Its first ride was a "gravity railroad" roller coaster, along with an oceanside pavilion for music and dancing that drew in guests. Playland truly began when it pioneered a fast photo-finishing process that allowed guests to take photos home that day. Business was bad during the Great Depression, so the owners of the park decided to buy up all the seaside attractions. The original owner died and it was then run by his son, but it was never the same. It was bought out by a millionaire developer in 1971, and torn down to build condominiums in 1972.

Attractions included Arthur Looff's "Bob Sled Dipper," the Looff-designed Big Dipper, the Shoot-the-chutes, the carousel, Aeroplane Swing, The Whip, Dodg'Em, the Ship of Joy, the Ferris wheel, Noah's Ark, and almost 100 concessionaires ("Playland (San Francisco)," 2016).

Playland Not-at-the-Beach
10979 San Pablo Avenue
El Cerrito CA 94530
(510) 592-3002
playland-not-at-the-beach.org

This indoor attraction has some artifacts from Whitney's Playland in San Francisco, according to its website (Playland, 2017).

Bohemian Club

624 Taylor Street
San Francisco CA 94102
(415) 885-2440

Motto: "Weaving spiders come not here."

Significance: Walt Disney was invited to the annual retreat in a redwood grove north of San Francisco Bay. However, he could not sleep all night due to the snores coming from other tents. This experience led to the creation of the snoring sequence in *Snow White and the Seven Dwarfs* ("Bohemian club," 2016). Owls, which were symbols in the club, appear frequently in the movie.

Background

The Bohemian Club was established in 1872 as a private club. In the 1800s, 'bohemian' was a synonym for 'newspaper writer.' The club began as journalists and artists, then grew to accept musicians, businessmen, and entrepreneurs. Members were established as successful, respectable family men. George H. and W. Bush, Ronald Reagan, David Rockefeller, Dick Cheney, and Richard Nixon, are only a few distinguished members of the Club ("Bohemian club," 2016).

Treasure Island
San Francisco CA 94130

Site of the 1939-1940 Golden Gate International Exposition

Significance: Walt Disney attended the Exposition in 1939. It was here where he found his love for miniatures. He looked at the dollhouses by Mrs. James Ward Thorne with much respect. The influence of miniatures is also shown in his work on the Carolwood Pacific, Walt's own small scale railroad around his home. Throughout the rest of his life, Disney continued to collect miniatures from all over the U.S. and Europe. (There is a collection of miniatures at the Art Institute of Chicago – see page 191.)

The Golden Gate International Exposition was held in 1939 and 1940 at Treasure Island. It was a World's Fair in celebration of the city's newly built bridges, the Oakland Bay and Golden Gate Bridges. The Exposition became known for its architecture, art, and brilliant lighting.

"Walt, along with fifteen animators and sketch artists, was there [Golden Gate International Exposition], February 17-21 in 1939, in part to attend a concert of the San Francisco Symphony Orchestra conducted by Leopold Stokowski. These artists were working on the early stages of what became *Fantasia*" (Smith, 2012, p. 246).

Bank of America
Address Unknown
San Francisco CA

Significance: Walt and Roy Disney traveled to the Bank of America board of directors meeting to answer questions about their loan, which increased to $4 million in the 1940s (Thomas, 1994).

"One day Joe Rosenberg, the bank's Los Angeles liaison with the studio, telephoned Roy to request that he and Walt answer questions about their loan at the board of directors meeting in San Francisco. In later years Roy enjoyed recounting the story of how he and Walt traveled north in a state of gloom. They had never before been summoned to a command appearance before the board" (Thomas, 1994, p. 186-187).

Bank of America had a branch at Disneyland from 1955 to 1993. From 1966 to 1992, it sponsored "It's a Small World" there (Smith, 2006).

To read Bank of America's story about working with Walt Disney: about.bankofamerica.com/en-us/our-story/building-a-small-world.html

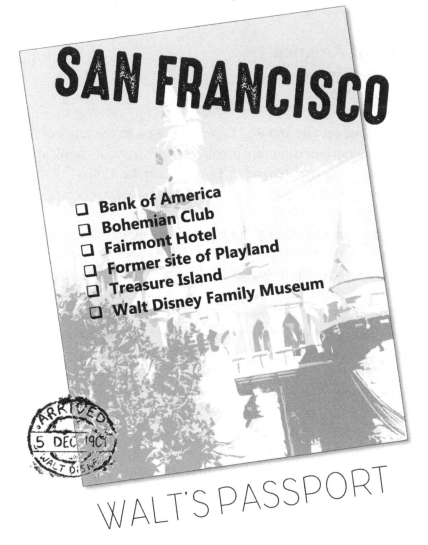

SAN FRANCISCO

- ☐ Bank of America
- ☐ Bohemian Club
- ☐ Fairmont Hotel
- ☐ Former site of Playland
- ☐ Treasure Island
- ☐ Walt Disney Family Museum

WALT'S PASSPORT

Chapter 20
Santa Barbara, California

All Saints by-the-Sea Episcopal Church

83 Eucalyptus Lane
Santa Barbara CA 93108
allsaintsbythesea.org
(805) 969-4771
info@asbts.org

Significance: The small church where Walt Disney walked his daughter Diane Disney down the aisle to marry Ron Miller on May 9, 1954 (This Day in Disney History, 2017).

Diane and Ron were baptized there the week before and Walt and Lillian served as their witnesses (Thomas, 1994).

Sharon Disney returned from the University of Arizona to serve as the maid of honor.

Biltmore Hotel

1260 Channel Drive
Santa Barbara CA 93108
(805) 969-2261
fourseasons.com/santabarbara

Significance: The site of Diane Disney and Ron Miller's wedding reception on May 9, 1954. The reception took place in the Loggia Room in the Biltmore Hotel.

"The Santa Barbara Biltmore (also known as the Biltmore) opened in 1927 as part of the Biltmore Hotels chain. Now styled as the Four Seasons Resort—The Biltmore Santa Barbara, it is a luxury hotel located in Santa Barbara, California. Its landmark

Spanish Colonial Revival architecture and gardens are on the Pacific Coast in Southern California, in the United States (Santa Barbara Biltmore, 2017, n.p.).

 Tour the hotel's elegant public areas. A must see.

SANTA BARBARA

☐ **All Saints-by-the-Sea Episcopal Church**
☐ **Biltmore Hotel**

ARRIVED 5 DEC 1901 WALT DISNEY

WALT'S PASSPORT

Chapter 21
Santa Monica, California

Providence St. John's Hospital

2121 Santa Monica Boulevard
Santa Monica CA 90404
(310) 829-5511
california.providence.org/saint-johns

Significance: In 1966, Walt entered this hospital due to a kidney ailment (Thomas, 1994).

SANTA MONICA

☐ **Providence St. John's Hospital**

ARRIVED
5 DEC 1901
WALT DISNEY

WALT'S PASSPORT

Chapter 22
Toluca Lake, California

Former home of Flora and Elias Disney, Walt's parents

4605 Placidia Avenue
Toluca Lake CA 91602

Significance: There is where Walt's parents lived. In 1936, Walt and Roy bought this house (for $8,300) for their parents for their 50th anniversary (Madden, 2017). Walt and Roy also paid to furnish this house (Madden, 2017). Unfortunately, this is where Flora Call Disney died on November 26, 1938 at the age of 70 (*Los Angeles Times*, November 27, 1938).

Home of
Roy O. Disney, Roy E. Disney, and Roy P. Disney

4311 Forman Avenue
Toluca Lake CA 91602

Significance: Roy O. Disney is the brother of Walt Disney. The house was passed onto Walt's nephew (Roy E. Disney) and grand-nephew (Roy P. Disney).

Related Information:
Sheri and Roy P. Disney contributed $1 million to the integrative medicine program. Roy P. Disney's parents, the late Roy E. Disney and Patricia Disney, donated $10 million on behalf of their family to the new Providence Saint Joseph Medical Center free-standing cancer center: Roy and Patricia Disney Family Cancer Center at Providence Saint Joseph Medical Center (*The Toluca Times*, January 27, 2010).

TOLUCA LAKE

☐ **Flora & Elias Home**
☐ **Roy Disneys' Home**

ARRIVED 5 DEC 1901 WALT DISNEY

WALT'S PASSPORT

Chapter 23
Three Rivers, California
and Mineral King area

Three Rivers Historical Society Museum
and Visitor Center

42268 Sierra Drive
Three Rivers CA 93271
(559) 561-2707
3Rmuseum.org

Significance: This museum and visitor
center has a Mineral King room with a corner dedicated to "The
Disney Dream."

Three Rivers Historical Society was officially established by the
State of California on December 17, 1991. The Historical
Museum and Visitors Center was established and opened on
October 19, 2000 (Three Rivers Historical Museum, 2017).
The Mineral King Room opened on January 22, 2017.

In this corner, you will find newspaper clippings about the
proposed Mineral King Ski Resort, photographs, and other
artifacts related to the project.

Check out this video:
"The Story of Walt Disney and Mineral King"
told by Bob Hicks:
tularecountytreasures.org/mineral-king.html

Hicks was the manager of the Mineral King project for Disney.

Mineral King

(within Sequoia National Park)
Sierra Nevada Mountains
Mineral King CA 93271
mineralking.org

Open Late May through
October (weather permitting)

Significance: This is where
Walt almost built a ski resort.

This is a 25-mile road through the mountains and will take about
2 hours.

"When I first saw Mineral King, I thought it was one of the most
beautiful places in the world, and we want to keep it that way.
With its development we will prove once again that man and
nature can work together to the benefit of both," stated Walt
Disney (Smith, 1994, p. 69).

"A steep, winding road leads to a place of rugged beauty:
Mineral King Valley. At 7800 feet (2375 m), it's the highest place
you can go in these parks by vehicle. The Mineral King subalpine
valley consists of both dense forests of pine, sequoia, and fir and
colorful granite and shale landscapes" (National Park Service,
April 24, 2017, n.p.).

Walt won a bid for private development offered by the United
States government in the 1960s. However, critics and
environmentalists raised concerns and Congress made Mineral
King a part of Sequoia National Park in 1978 (Smith, 2006).

There is a small cabin with Disney-related items.

The Walt Disney Company still owns land in Mineral King, but can never build on it.

 Mineral King webcam:
mk-webcam.net

Planning Your Visit:

 I recommend that you have lunch at the Silver City Resort restaurant (open Thursdays through Mondays typically):

silvercityresort.com/about-silver-city/restaurant-and-store

Do a Day Hike in Mineral King:
nps.gov/seki/planyourvisit/mkdayhikesum.htm

Overnight Accommodations

Silver City Resort (2 night minimum stay required):
silvercityresort.com

Camping: 2 Seasonal Campgrounds
Atwell Mill Campground
Cold Springs Campground
Available on a first-come, first-serve basis
nps.gov/seki/planyourvisit/mineralkingcg.htm

Bring sunscreen and bug spray!

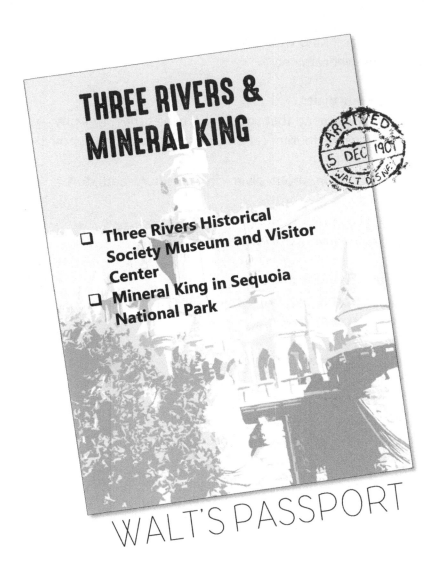

THREE RIVERS & MINERAL KING

ARRIVED
5 DEC 1901
WALT DISNE

- ☐ Three Rivers Historical Society Museum and Visitor Center
- ☐ Mineral King in Sequoia National Park

WALT'S PASSPORT

Chapter 24
Valencia, California

California Institute of the Arts (CalArts)

24700 McBean Parkway
Valencia CA 91355
(661) 255-1050
calarts.edu

 Located 30 miles
north of
Los Angeles

Significance: Walt founded this four-year postsecondary school, which opened in 1971, five years after his death.

 Watch a video about CalArts:
calarts.edu/about/institute/history

CalArts offers education in six schools: Art, Critical Studies, Dance, Film/Video, Music, and Theater.

Walt "sent researchers across the country to visit art schools and conservatories, studying the curricula and facilities, measuring classrooms and corridor space. Walt sought advice from such administrators as Lee DuBridge of Caltech and Franklin Murphy of UCLA. He commissioned his own artists to create brochures and sketches of prospective campuses"
(Thomas, 1994, p. 330-331).

"The institute was started as Disney's dream of an interdisciplinary 'Caltech of the arts,' with all schools under one roof. The initial concept behind CalArts' interdisciplinary approach came from Richard Wagner's idea of Gesamtkunstwerk ('total artwork'), which Disney himself was fond of and explored in a variety of forms, beginning with his own studio, then later in the incorporation of CalArts" (Disney Wiki, n.d., n.p.).

Thirty seven locations were considered for CalArts (Thomas, 1994).

A large bequest from Walt's estate helped to finance the construction of CalArts (Smith, 2006). Fifty acres were acquired from Newhall Land and Farming for the campus (Thomas, 1998).

Timeline
calarts.edu/about/institute/history/timeline (CalArts, n.d.b)

1960
Walt Disney develops plans for a new school for the performing and visual arts where different creative disciplines come together under one roof, inspiring and elevating each other.

1961
Walt Disney and his brother, Roy O. Disney, guide the merger of the Los Angeles Conservatory of Music, founded in 1883, and the Chouinard Art Institute, founded in 1921, to form California Institute of the Arts. The Disney brothers are joined in this undertaking by Lulu May Von Hagen, chair of the Conservatory.

1964
The Institute—dubbed "CalArts," following the example of "Caltech"—is introduced to the public by Walt Disney at the Hollywood premiere of *Mary Poppins*. He envisions a campus in the hills overlooking Hollywood's Cahuenga Pass.

1966
Following Walt Disney's death, his plans for CalArts proceed with the support of the Disney family and other benefactors. When Walt died, the family requested that contributions be made to CalArts, instead of flowers.

1971
With some classes having already moved to Valencia during the spring, the permanent campus opens in full for the start of fall semester, welcoming more than 650 students.

1997:
As plans take shape for the construction of the Frank O. Gehry-designed Walt Disney Concert Hall in downtown Los Angeles, longtime benefactors Roy E. and Patty Disney provide initial funding for a separate CalArts performance space and gallery: the Roy and Edna Disney/CalArts Theater (REDCAT), so named in memory of Roy E. Disney's parents. The venue would at last give the Institute a presence in the heart of the city—as originally intended by Walt Disney.

In 2004, The Sharon Disney Lund School of Dance is dedicated in memory of the longstanding CalArts benefactor and Walt's youngest daughter.

WALT DISNEY MODULAR THEATRE

Walt Disney Modular Theatre
"Shared among the Institute's Schools, this vast black-box theater provides a venue for major operatic, world music, and other ensemble performances. It possesses a variable architecture that supports an unlimited range of stage and audience configurations" (CalArts School of Music, n.d., n.p.).

The 1993 Restoration of the Theatre was supported by Mrs. Walter E. Disney (Lillian Disney).

Roy O. Disney Music Hall (ROD)
Dedicated December 7, 1975

"Many on-campus performances take place in the Roy O. Disney Music Hall (ROD), a multipurpose space with adaptable acoustics, lighting, and sound features. The ROD supports traditional recitals and concerts as well as multimedia and other experimental presentations. The space also doubles as a live recording room, equipped with its own assortment of recording-quality microphones and gear" (CalArts School of Music, n.d., n.p.).

Sharon Disney Lund School of Dance and Theater
Dedicated in 2004

"The Sharon Disney Lund Dance Theater is a 50-foot-by-70-foot space used exclusively for dance performances, rehearsals and classes. This hall features state of the art wall-to-wall L'Air sprung flooring covered with seamless black Lonstage. Retractable theater seating allows for many different staging configurations. Seating capacity is usually 100 to 125 persons, with a maximum capacity of 250"
(CalArts School of Dance, n.d., n.p.).

Patty Disney Center for Life and Work
Dedicated in September 2014

This space is used for Career Services offices, some Community Arts Partnership offices, Art Change US, two big classrooms/conference spaces and one small meeting space. Patty Disney was the wife of Roy E. Disney, nephew of Walt Disney.

Disney Family Affiliations

Chairman of the Board:
Tim Disney, Walt's grandnephew

Member of the Board of Trustees:
Michelle Lund, President, The Sharon D. Lund Foundation
Daughter of Sharon Disney Lund/Granddaughter of Walt Disney

Trustee Emeritus:
William S. Lund, son-in-law of Walt Disney

Former President of CalArts:
William S. Lund, son-in-law of Walt Disney

Donors: Various members of the Disney family

Affiliated: REDCAT
Roy and Edna Disney/CalArts Theater

"Roy Disney and his wife Patty personally matched the Disney Company gift for REDCAT construction, extending Roy's history of more than three decades of support and continuing the work of his father, who had not only been Walt's partner in building The Walt Disney Company, but had also overseen the construction of CalArts' Valencia campus. Roy and Patty chose to permanently dedicate REDCAT to the memory of Roy's parents

131

by naming it the Roy and Edna Disney/CalArts Theater. It is a fitting tribute: the names of Walt and Roy Disney will remain side by side in perpetuity" (REDCAT, 2016). For more information about REDCAT, see page 69.

Note: Newhall, CA and Valencia, CA are nearby so you should check out both cities together. (See Chapter 9: Newhall, CA).

Additional Background Information
The first year of classes were held at Villa Cabrini, a former Catholic girls school in Burbank, California (Thomas, 1998).

In the early days, there were challenges of students swimming nude, thievery, and marijuana (Thomas, 1998). Because of those challenges and the cost of running CalArts, Roy O. Disney explored selling CalArts to the University of Southern California (USC). However, that deal fell through, as did an attempt to work with Pepperdine University (Thomas, 1998).

VALENCIA

☐ **California Institute of the Arts (CalArts)**

ARRIVED
5 DEC 1961
WALT DISNEY

WALT'S PASSPORT

Chapter 25
West Hollywood, California

Chasen's Restaurant

Now the site of Bristol Farms Grocery Store
9039 Beverly Boulevard
West Hollywood CA 90048
bristolfarms.com/location/west-hollywood

Significance: Walt and Lillian Disney would dine there on occasion (Thomas, 1994).

"Chasen's was a restaurant frequented by entertainers in West Hollywood, California. Located at 9039 Beverly Boulevard on the border of Beverly Hills, it first opened for business in 1936 and was the site for many years of the Academy Awards party. The original building, save the Beverly Blvd. facing wall, was demolished and a Bristol Farms grocery store was built in its place. In the cafe of this grocery store are several booths from the original Chasen's and some of the original paneling" (Chasen's, n.d., n.p.).

WEST HOLLYWOOD

☐ **Chasen's Restaurant/ Bristol Farms**

ARRIVED
5 DEC 190?
WALT DISNE?

WALT'S PASSPORT

Chapter 26
Yosemite, California

Ahwahnee Hotel

(now the Majestic Yosemite Hotel)
1 Ahwahnee Drive
Yosemite National Park CA 95389
(888) 413-8869
travelyosemite.com/lodging/the-majestic-yosemite-hotel/

Significance: At Christmas in 1935, Walt took his family there. Walt and Lillian ice skated there. Diane was only 2 years old and they were accompanied by Diane's nurse, Ada Alexander (Walt Disney Family Museum photo caption).

COLORADO

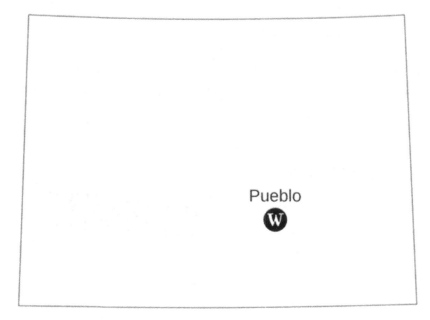

Pueblo

 Food Available

 Guided Tour Available

 Not Open to the Public

 Original Structure Gone

 Train Connection

 Parking Fee

 Post Death Tribute

 Hotel

 Must See

 Multimedia

 Admission Fee

 Drive By Location

Chapter 27
Pueblo, Colorado

 Significance: While working as a news butcher for the Van Noy Interstate News Company, Walt traveled as far west on the train to Pueblo, Colorado.

"When we arrived in Pueblo [likely at the Union Depot] and disembarked to find a hotel for the night, a salesman Walt had met on the train...handed him a card with the address of a boarding house which he highly recommended" (Silvester, 2014, p. 38). Walt realized he was at a brothel and quickly left.

CONNECTICUT

W New Haven

W Sound Beach

Food Available   Guided Tour Available   Not Open to the Public   Original Structure Gone   Train Connection   Parking Fee

Post Death Tribute   Hotel   Must See   Multimedia   Admission Fee   Drive By Location

Chapter 28
Sound Beach, Connecticut

Camp King
Ye Old Greenwich Inn
(now today's Old Greenwich)
Shore Road

It burned down in 1925.

Significance: Walt reported here in Fall 1918 when serving in the American Ambulance Corps.

"In November 1918, Walt was sent to Camp King at Sound Beach, Connecticut. Camp King was located on Long Island Sound, at Ye Old Greenwich Inn on Greenwich Point, a mile south of present-day downtown Old Greenwich. The inn was described by Sgt. Wilson as 'a large wooden building and well furnished hotel which had closed for the season,' and had been leased to the Red Cross "to house the boys until sent overseas" (Apgar, April 6, 2016, n.p.).

"Walt rarely spoke about his experience at Camp King, which lasted two short weeks. Although in an interview in the mid-1950s with an early biographer, Pete Martin, a writer and editor with the *The Saturday Evening Post*, he joked about 'spending half the time' at Sound Beach in the guardhouse, and on kitchen patrol, as punishment 'for just clowning'" (Apgar, April 6, 2016, n.p.).

According to Dave Smith (2012), Walt Disney and Ray Kroc (American businessman who made McDonald's famous and successful) both trained here before heading to France.

To learn more about Walt's time in the American Ambulance Corps., read *In the Service of the Red Cross* by David Lesjak. Available from Theme Park Press.

Chapter 29
New Haven, Connecticut

Yale University

Woolsey Hall
New Haven CT 06520
(203) 432-4771
yale.edu

Significance: On June 22, 1938, Walt received a Master of Arts honorary degree from Yale University in Woolsey Hall (Barrier, 2015). See pages 77, 81, and 207-208 for his other honorary degrees.

"Walt was in distinguished company: among his fellow honorees were Lord Tweedsmuir, the governor general of Canada—better known as the novelist and biographer John Buchan—and Justice Stanley Reed of the U.S. Supreme Court, who both received honorary doctor of laws degrees, and the great German novelist Thomas Mann, who received a doctor of letters degree" (Barrier, 2015, n.p.).

"Yale's then-new president, Charles Seymour, responded by saying as he bestowed Walt's degree:

> Creator of a new language of art, who has brought the joy of deep laughter to millions and, by touching the heart of humanity without distinction of race, has served as ambassador of international good-will, Yale confers upon you the degree of master of arts, admitting you to all its rights and privileges" (Barrier, 2015, n.p.).

NEW HAVEN

ARRIVED
5 DEC. 1901
WALT DISNEY

☐ **Yale University**

WALT'S PASSPORT

FLORIDA

Altoona

Bay Lake, Lake Buena Vista, Ocoee & Orlando

Key West

Food Available	Guided Tour Available	Not Open to the Public	Original Structure Gone	Train Connection	Parking Fee
Post Death Tribute	Hotel	Must See	Multimedia	Admission Fee	Drive By Location

Chapter 30
Altoona, Florida

Ponceannah Cemetery
County Road 42
Altoona FL 32702
(approximate address: 23825 County Road 42)

Located about 52 miles north of Walt Disney World Resort

Burial Site of Walt Disney's Maternal Grandparents

Charles Call's Gravesite
Date of Death: January 6, 1890
Significance: Charles was Walt Disney's grandfather.
Charles' daughter was Flora Call, Walt's mother.

Henrietta Gross Call's Gravesite
Date of Death: February 21, 1910
Significance: Henrietta was Walt's grandmother and mother to Flora Call, Walt's mother.

Location of their grave:
Back of cemetery with tall, white, stone round monument

ALTOONA

ARRIVED
5 DEC 1901
WALT DISNEY

☐ **Burial site of Walt Disney's Maternal Grandparents**

WALT'S PASSPORT

Chapter 31
Bay Lake, Florida

Bay Lake, Florida 32830

No specific location.

Significance: This is a city owned by the Walt Disney Company through Reedy Creek Improvement District (RCID) (see pages 159-160 for more information on Reedy Creek). Because Walt was planning to build EPCOT as an experimental city, the Florida government authorized the formation of this city within the Walt Disney Company control (Lake Buena Vista, FL is similar – see Chapter 33). Bay Lake is a city recognized in Orange County Florida and is named after Bay Lake, which is just east of the Magic Kingdom. In 2010, the population of Bay Lake was 47 (Bay Lake, n.d.).

"The only residents of the city are Disney employees and their immediate family members who live in a community on the north shore of Bay Lake (on Bay Court). The only landowners are fully owned subsidiaries of The Walt Disney Company, rights-of-way for state and county roads, and five five-acre lots owned by senior Disney employees to give them voting power in the Reedy Creek Improvement District" (Bay Lake, n.d.).

BAY LAKE

ARRIVED
5 DEC 1901
WALT DISNEY

□ **Bay Lake area**

WALT'S PASSPORT

Chapter 32
Key West, Florida

No specific location.

 Significance: In 1930, Walt and Lillian, as part of their vacation, took a train from Washington, D.C. to Key West. In Key West, they boarded a ship for Cuba (Thomas, 1994).

KEY WEST

☐ **Key West area**

ARRIVED 5 DEC 1901 WALT DISNEY

WALT'S PASSPORT

Chapter 33
Lake Buena Vista, Florida

Compilation of information assisted by Emily Fackler

Walt Disney World Resort

1180 Seven Seas Drive
Lake Buena Vista FL 32830
(407) 939-5277
disneyworld.disney.go.com

Significance: Walt's second theme park and one that bears his first name, which was insisted by his brother, Roy.

This Florida destination was referred to as "Project X" in the beginning. See EPCOT section on pages 158-159 for more information about Walt's original vision.

Walt's last visit to view the Florida property was in May 1966 (Smith, 2012).

Magic Kingdom

1180 Seven Seas Drive
Lake Buena Vista FL 32830
disneyworld.disney.go.com/destinations/magic-kingdom/

Opened October 1, 1971 (Smith, 2006).

"Believe me, it's the most exciting and challenging assignment we have ever tackled at Walt Disney Productions," said Walt Disney, referring to Walt Disney World (Smith, 1994, p. 95).

MAIN STREET, U.S.A.

There is a window that reads: "Magic Kingdom Casting Agency – 'It takes People to Make the Dream a Reality' – Walter Elias Disney, Founder & Director Emeritus." It is located above the Main Street Cinema (an identical window is located in Disneyland's Main Street, U.S.A.). The window is dedicated to Disney cast members (personal communication, D. Smith, July 5, 2017).

 Railroad Station
Above the Railroad Station, a window reads: "Walt Disney World Railroad Office – Keeping Dreams on Track – Walter E. Disney, Chief Engineer."

 Walt Disney World Railroad
disneyworld.disney.go.com/attractions/magic-kingdom/walt-disney-world-railroad/

This is a 20-minute, 1.5 mile ride around the Magic Kingdom. Three of the four train cars are named for Disney family members: Walter E. Disney, Lilly Belle (a tribute to Lillian Disney), and Roy O. Disney (a tribute to Walt's brother) (Walt Disney World, n.d.a). For more information about the Lilly Belle, see page 28.

CENTRAL HUB

Partners Statue
Located in the Hub in front of the Castle

This statue of Walt Disney with Mickey Mouse was installed in 1995, two years after the 1993 installation in Disneyland (WESH2, December 10, 2014). It was created by sculptor Blaine Gibson (Korkis, 2011).

The Partners Statue also appears in Disneyland, the Disney Legends Plaza, Tokyo Disneyland, and The Walt Disney Studios Park in Paris. For more information, see page 30.

TOMORROWLAND

Walt Disney's Carousel of Progress
"Walt Disney's Carousel of Progress was personally created by Walt Disney for the 1964-65 New York World's Fair (see pages 282-284). Featuring state-of-the-art Audio-Animatronics—Walt Disney's latest animation technology at the time—the show was originally conceived as part of a new area at Disneyland park called Edison Square. When the concept was abandoned, the idea was re-imagined, eventually opening under the name [General Electric's] 'Progressland,' [featuring the Carousel of Progress] at the 1964-65 New York World's Fair. With the classic song 'There's a Great Big Beautiful Tomorrow,' written and composed by the Academy Award®-winning team of brothers Richard and Robert Sherman, the show was an instant hit. Following its success, the show moved to Disneyland park and was renamed 'The Carousel of Progress,' where it played until September 9, 1973. In January 15, 1975, the attraction moved to [the] Magic Kingdom theme park where it was rewritten and restaged with a new theme song, "The Best Time of Your Life." But in the true spirit of progress, the show was reworked in 1994 to its initial incarnation with the original theme song intact—as a

tribute to nostalgia" (Walt Disney's Carousel of Progress, n.d., n.p.).

Walt Disney: From Marceline to the Magic Kingdom
A Tour in the Magic Kingdom
disneyworld.disney.go.com/events-tours/magic-kingdom/marceline-to-magic-kingdom/
(407) WDW-TOUR

A 3-hour tour
Recommended for ages 12 and up

"Step back in time for a 'behind-the-scenes' glimpse into some of the secrets behind the magic. Your knowledgeable guide will share many little-known facts about Walt's upbringing in Marceline, Missouri as well as provide insider info about the design and operation of several classic attractions, including those inspired by Walt's participation in the 1964 World's Fair" (see pages 282-284) (Walt Disney World, n.d.b, n.p.).

100 Years of Magic
In 2001 (through 2003), to honor Walt Disney's 100th birthday, this special celebration at Walt Disney World was held. This included four special parades (Share a Dream Come True, Tapestry of Dreams, Mickey's Jammin' Jungle, and Stars and Motor Cars (Smith, 2006).

Disney's Hollywood Studios

Walt Disney Presents
Animation Courtyard
disneyworld.disney.go.com/attractions/hollywood-studios/walt-disney-one-mans-dream/

In August 2017, the Walt Disney World Resort announced that "One Man's Dream" was being redone and becoming "Walt Disney Presents": "[This] will continue showcasing historic items from Walt Disney's history, such as sketches, photos and storyboards. But wait – Walt Disney Presents will also act as a preview center where guests explore what's next for the park" (Fickley-Baker, August 11, 2017, n.p.).

As One Man's Dream, this was an exhibit full of Walt artifacts and film clips that tell the story of Walt's life. It included a 15-minute movie about Walt Disney narrated by Julie Andrews. One Man's Dream was originally created to commemorate the 100th anniversary of Walt's birth in 2001.

The new marquee features this tagline:
"From Mickey Mouse to the Magic Kingdoms and Beyond"

Tribute to Holly Vermont Realty
On a door in Disney's Hollywood Studios is a logo for "Holly Vermont Realty," which pays tribute to the first studio space Walt used (see page 73) (WDW Radio, January 24, 2013).

EPCOT
(Experimental Prototype Community of Tomorrow)
Walt Disney World Resort

200 Epcot Center Drive
Orlando FL 32821
disneyworld.disney.go.com/destinations/epcot

The EPCOT that Walt had envisioned is not what EPCOT is today. Instead, EPCOT is one of the four theme parks in the Walt Disney World Resort.

When Walt acquired the Florida property, he wanted to his build his own perfect Utopian city.

"It's like the city of tomorrow ought to be. A city that caters to the people as a service function. It will be a planned, controlled community, a showcase for American industry and research, schools, cultural and educational opportunities,"
stated Walt Disney (Smith, 1994, p. 52).

"Walt's original vision of E.P.C.O.T was for a model community, home to twenty thousand residents, which would be a test bed for city planning and organization. The community was to have been built in the shape of a circle, with businesses and commercial areas at its center, community buildings and schools and recreational complexes around it, and residential neighborhoods along the perimeter. Transportation would have been provided by monorails and PeopleMovers (like the one in the Magic Kingdom's Tomorrowland). Automobile traffic would be kept underground, leaving pedestrians safe above-ground. Walt Disney said, 'It will be a planned, controlled community, a showcase for American industry and research, schools, cultural and educational opportunities. In E.P.C.O.T., there will be no slum areas because we won't let them develop. There will be no landowners and therefore no voting control. People will rent houses instead of buying them, and at modest rentals. There will

be no retirees; everyone must be employed'"
(Walt Disney's Original E.P.C.O.T., n.d., n.p.).

 Watch Walt's introduction of EPCOT:
Search "Virtual 360° View of Walt Disney's EPCOT City -
DisneyAvenue.com" on YouTube

Reedy Creek Improvement District (RCID)

Administration Office
1900 Hotel Plaza Boulevard
Lake Buena Vista FL 32830
(407) 828–2241
rcid.org

Significance: A special taxing district that Walt Disney arranged
with the State of Florida.

The 92-page District Charter is on the RCID website.

"Reedy Creek Improvement District (the "District") is a
progressive form of government, created in 1967 by a special
Act of the Florida Legislature, the purpose of which is to support
and administer certain aspects of the economic development
and tourism within District boundaries. With an administration
office located on Hotel Plaza Boulevard in Lake Buena Vista, the
District encompasses approximately 25,000 acres in both Orange
and Osceola counties, servicing 19 landowners, including Walt
Disney Co. and its wholly-owned affiliates" (RCID, 2016a, n.p.).

"Chapter 67-764 of the Laws of Florida was signed into law by
Governor Claude R. Kirk, Jr. on May 12, 1967, creating the
District. On the same day, Governor Kirk also signed the
incorporation acts for two cities inside the District: Bay Lake
(Chapter 67-1104) and Reedy Creek (Chapter 67-1965). (The City

of Reedy Creek was renamed to the City of Lake Buena Vista around 1970)" (RCID, n.d., n.p.).

"In the mid-1960s, the Walt Disney World Company proposed building a recreation-oriented development on 25,000 acres of property in Central Florida. The property sat in a remote area of Orange and Osceola County, so secluded that the nearest power and water lines were 10-15 miles away. Neither Orange nor Osceola County had the services or the resources needed to bring the project to life.

In 1967 the Florida State legislature, working with Walt Disney World Company, created a special taxing district – called the Reedy Creek Improvement District – that would act with the same authority and responsibility as a county government.

Walt Disney World could then move ahead with its vision to turn 38.5 square miles of largely uninhabited pasture and swamp land into a global destination resort that welcomes millions of visitors every year.

The new legislation said that landowners within the Reedy Creek Improvement District, primarily Walt Disney World, would be solely responsible for paying the cost of providing typical municipal services like power, water, roads, fire protection, etc.

Local taxpayers, meaning residents of Orange and Osceola County, would not have to pay for building or maintaining those services" (RCID, 2016b, n.p.).

Disney Springs: Empress Lilly (now Paddlefish)

The Landing
1486 Buena Vista Drive
Orlando FL 32830
disneyworld.disney.go.com/dining/disney-springs/paddlefish/

Significance: Empress Lilly was named after Walt's wife, Lillian (Lilly) (Smith, 2006).

Disney's Grand Floridian Resort

4401 Floridian Way
Orlando FL 32830
(407) 824-3000
disneyworld.disney.go.com/resorts/grand-floridian-resort-and-spa

 Walt Disney Suite (Room 4411, 4th Floor)

Significance: A 1,690-square-foot suite named after Walt Disney. It is one of the four signature suites at this resort. There is also a suite named after Roy O. Disney.

 The hotel suite is located in the main building of the Resort on the Club Level. This suite is filled with memorabilia about Walt, including his interest in railroads. This suite includes a living room, dining room, bedroom, a second bedroom, and a spacious balcony.

To read more about the creation of Walt Disney World, check out *Project Future* by Chad Denver Emerson.

LAKE BUENA VISTA

- ☐ Disney Springs: Empress Lilly
- ☐ Disney's Grand Floridian Resort
- ☐ Disney's Hollywood Studios
- ☐ EPCOT
- ☐ Magic Kingdom
- ☐ Reedy Creek Improvement District

ARRIVED
5 DEC 1901
WALT DISN

WALT'S PASSPORT

Chapter 34
Ocoee, Florida

Site of the Former Ramada Inn & Former Colony Plaza Hotel

11100 West Colonial Drive
Ocoee FL 34761

Significance: Site of the April 30, 1969 press conference to provide details about Walt Disney World.

"As someone put it, a 'giant circus tent' was set up outside the hotel and invited guests were able to preview the upcoming opening of Walt Disney World Resort. Roy Disney, along with Disney legends Card Walker, John Hench, Charlie Ridgway, and Donn Tatum signed autographs and...announced October 1, 1971 as the opening date. Roy told guests at the event:

'You should know that the dedication of our staff to Walt's goals is tremendous. And I know Walt would like what his creative team is doing because these are the ideas and plans he began. Everything you will see here today is something Walt worked on and began in some way. And today, the Walt Disney organization is dedicated to carrying out these wonderful plans in Walt Disney World'" (Built, 2017, n.p.).

"Anybody who was anybody in the state that helped Disney set up their kingdom was brought to that hotel," recalls Ocoee Mayor Scott Vandergrift, then a city commissioner. "It [the hotel] was as nice as anything Orlando had at the time" (Mathers, April 14, 2005, n.p.).

Donn B. Tatum, president of Walt Disney World Co. in 1969, concluded the press conference with this statement: "The preparations for Walt Disney World have been comprehensive and deliberate, always with the goal in mind of providing for our visitors the most extensive and exciting vacation attraction ever planned by a single corporation. A solid foundation has been achieved, and construction is ready to move forward" (Walt Disney World Press Release, April 30, 1969, p. 1).

The building was demolished in May, 2009.

□ Site of former Colony Plaza Hotel

Chapter 35
Orlando, Florida

Compilation of information assisted by Emily Fackler

Walt Disney Amphitheater
Lake Eola Park

Downtown Orlando
512 East Washington Street
Orlando FL 32801
(407) 246-4484
cityoforlando.net/parks/lake-eola-park

Built in 1989

"The Walt Disney Amphitheater was donated to the City of
Orlando by The Walt Disney Company in 1989. An outdoor
venue and stage, it's an excellent site for public events,
community plays, dance performances, outdoor movie showings,
and free concerts. The look of the theatre reflects the beach
scene of 1950s Florida. The bandshell was built in a retro design
with a scallop-shaped facade, and from above, the amphitheater
seating also fans out from the bandshell in a scallop shape. The
theatre underwent a renovation in 2007 to improve the sound
and projection capabilities, and expanded its seating capacity to
1,157. This was done in the hopes of making the theatre more
available to bigger acts. The Walt Disney Amphitheater
complements the Lake Eola scene providing a great view of the
cityscape and the Lake Eola Fountain"
(Today's Orlando, 2013, n.p.).

Cherry Plaza Hotel

425 East Central Boulevard
Orlando FL 32801

Cherry Plaza Hotel is now currently the Post Parkside
Apartments.

Significance: Site of the November 15, 1965 press conference
to announce Walt Disney World.

Along Lake Eola, the Cherry Plaza Hotel was one of the tallest
buildings in Orlando when it was built in the 1950's. It was
originally called the Eola Plaza, but changed to the Cherry Plaza
Hotel in the 1960's. This was the most successful and most
interesting time for the plaza. During this time, important guests
visited and held their events in the Egyptian Room.

In 1964, Walt started purchasing small pieces of land in central
Florida. It was a great mystery to everyone in the world. They
were wondering what big corporation was buying the land,
especially since it was selling at only $185 an acre and it was
mostly swampland. An editor of the *Sunday Florida Magazine*,
Emily Bavar, was the first to predict it was Walt Disney. More
prominent newspapers began to publish and expand the story
including the *Star-Sentinel* and the *Orlando Sentinel*. General
William Potter, who Walt put in charge of the Florida Project,
was the first to see the paper and call California. It was time for a
press conference. Walt made a small announcement in Miami at
the Florida League of Municipalities Convention on October 25.
Walt made it known that "Walt Disney Productions will build the
greatest attraction yet known in the history of Florida." The
official press conference happened at the Cherry Plaza Hotel in
Orlando on November 15, 1965. The press conference included
Walt, his brother Roy, and the governor of Florida, Haydon
Burns. At the press conference, Burns discussed how Walt
Disney's project would be new, pleasurable, entertaining, and

economically satisfying. Walt only revealed that the new project will top Disneyland in California in size and in fantasy. He explained that they were in the planning process, and kept all the creative plans a secret. The only fact that he revealed was that the new facility would be in Florida. Governor Burns asked Walt several questions about the number of tourists it would attract, taxes, new roads and traffic, and the general impact that the Disney touch will have on Florida (Mahne, 2015).

 Watch the 18-minute video of the 1965 press conference. Search "Walt Disney 1965 WDW Press Conference - Project Florida - Full Video" on YouTube.

Metcalf Building
100 South Orange Avenue
Orlando FL 32801

Significance: "During the mid-1960's the Metcalf Building was the first Florida headquarters of the Disney Corporation as Walt Disney began the assemblage of Orlando area properties that became Disney World" (100 S. Orange Avenue, 2017, n.p.).

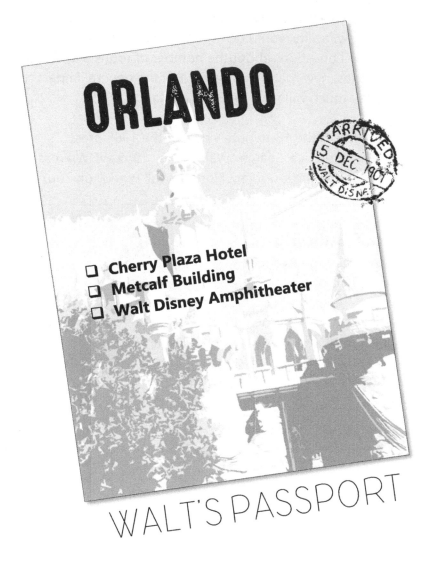

ORLANDO

ARRIVED
15 DEC 1901
WALT DISNEY

- ☐ **Cherry Plaza Hotel**
- ☐ **Metcalf Building**
- ☐ **Walt Disney Amphitheater**

WALT'S PASSPORT

HAWAII

Koloa

Honolulu
&
Waikiki

Significance: Walt and his family visited Hawaii four times in 1934, 1939, 1948, and 1965.

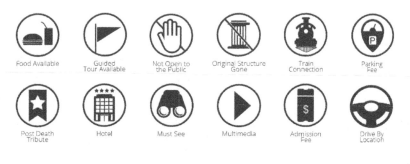

Food Available	Guided Tour Available	Not Open to the Public	Original Structure Gone	Train Connection	Parking Fee
Post Death Tribute	Hotel	Must See	Multimedia	Admission Fee	Drive By Location

Chapter 36
Island of Oahu
Honolulu, Hawaii

1934 Visit

"Walt and Lillian Disney made their first trip to Hawai'i in 1934, sailing on the Matson liner Lurline from Los Angeles (via the Port of San Francisco) on August 10. They arrived in Honolulu the morning of Thursday, August 16. Walt's arrival in the islands was big news, rating a headline at the top of the [Honolulu] Advertiser's August 17 front page, accompanied by photos of both Walt and Lilly, reports Disney scholar and biographer Michael Barrier" (Kurtti, n.d., n.p.).

"The Advertiser reported that, 'He had no sooner set foot ashore than he was besieged with invitations to go here, go there, meet this one, and do that for someone else.' Walt coyly replied, 'I don't want to do anything except lie on the beach in the sun and wiggle my toes in the sand'" (Kurtti, n.d., n.p.).

"He and Lilly were in Honolulu until the following Tuesday, attending a charity event on Saturday, August 18 (the opening game of the army's baseball championship series), an aerial acrobatics show performed by army pilots, and even a demonstration of modern antiaircraft equipment in the company of U.S. Army Brigadier General Robert S. Abernethy" (Kurtti, n.d., n.p.).

Princess Theatre

1236 Fort Street
Honolulu HI 96813

Liberty Theatre

1179 Nuuanu Avenue
Honolulu HI 96813

Significance: During his 1934 trip to Honolulu, Walt made a personal appearance before sold-out houses at two downtown Honolulu movie theatres — the Princess and the Liberty" (Kurtti, n.d., n.p.).

"The Disneys departed Honolulu on Saturday, August 25, 1934..." (Kurtti, n.d., n.p.).

1939 and 1949 Visit: Waikiki

Royal Hawaiian Resort

2259 Kalakaua Avenue
Honolulu HI 96815
(808) 923-7311
royal-hawaiian.com

Significance: "...In 1939, Walt and Lillian returned via the Lurline, and again stayed in Waikiki at the Royal Hawaiian. This time they were accompanied by Walt's brother, Roy, and his wife, Edna" (Kurtti, n.d., n.p.).

"Walt and Lilly, along with daughters Diane and Sharon, again sailed on the Lurline and enjoyed a family vacation at the Royal Hawaiian in 1948" (Kurtti, n.d., n.p.).

Chapter 37
Island of Kauai
Koloa, Hawaii

Waiohai Hotel

(now Marriott's Waiohai Beach Club)
2249 Poipu Road
Koloa HI 96756
(808) 742-4400
marriottvacationclub.com/vacation-resorts/marriott-waiohai-beach-club/overview.shtml

Significance: The Disney family visited the Island of Kauai to film the movie, *Lt. Robin Crusoe*, which starred Dick VanDyke.

"The Disney family made another Hawaiian visit for this occasion, departing for Kaua'i on May 7, 1965. 'The location was really a wonderful time for us,' Diane told Jim Korkis. 'We spent about three weeks at the Waiohai Hotel with mom and dad, Bill and Nolie Walsh, the Van Dykes, Byron Paul and his family. The Van Dykes were a wonderful family. Dick's a superb human being as well as a great talent'" (Kurtti, n.d., n.p.).

"The Waiohai had just opened in 1962, an assemblage of low-rise, two-story 'Polynesian cottages'" (Kurtti, n.d., n.p.).

"*Lt. Robin Crusoe USN* is a 1966 comedy film released and scripted by Walt Disney, and starring Dick Van Dyke as a U.S. Navy pilot who becomes a castaway on a tropical island" (Lt. Robin Crusoe, U.S.N., n.d., n.p.). "The story was loosely based on Daniel Defoe's classic novel *Robinson Crusoe*. It was Walt Disney's idea to make the adaptation, and this is the only film in which he received a story credit (as "Retlaw Yensid")" (Lt. Robin Crusoe, U.S.N., n.d., n.p.). Ron Miller co-produced it with Walt (Lt. Robin Crusoe, U.S.N., (n.d., n.p.).

Allerton Botanical Gardens

4425 Lawa'i Road
Koloa HI 96756
ntbg.org/gardens/allerton

Significance: The Gardens were used in this movie.

"The estate of Queen Lilu Kalani (the last reigning monarch of the Hawaiian Islands), was used for beach scenes. The 80-acre Allerton Botanical Gardens was the setting for the dense jungle through which Crusoe flees from a group of spear-wielding native girls" (Kurtti, n.d., n.p.).

Disney Hawaiian Connection:

Aulani Disney Resort & Spa
Ko Olina
Island of Oahu
disneyaulani.com

ARRIVED
5 DEC 1901
WALT DISNE.

HAWAII

HONOLULU
- ❑ Former site of Princess Theatre
- ❑ Former site of Liberty Theatre

WAIKIKI
- ❑ Royal Hawaiian Resort

KOLOA
- ❑ Waiohai Hotel
- ❑ Allerton Botanical Gardens

WALT'S PASSPORT

IDAHO

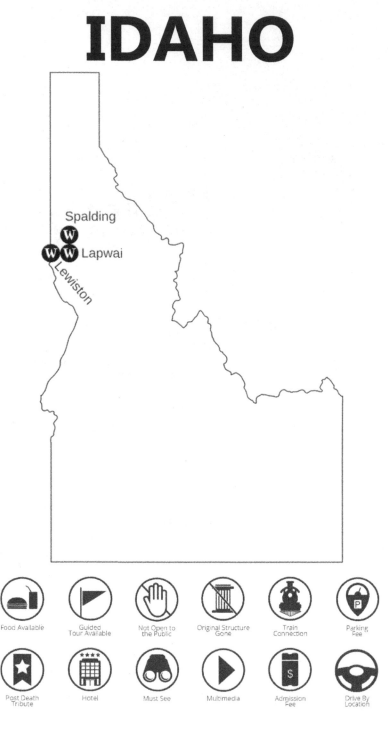

Spalding

Lapwai

Lewiston

Food Available	Guided Tour Available	Not Open to the Public
Original Structure Gone	Train Connection	Parking Fee
Post Death Tribute	Hotel	Must See
Multimedia	Admission Fee	Drive By Location

Chapter 38
Lapwai, Idaho

Lapwai Middle/High School

200 Willow Avenue West
Lapwai ID 83540
(208) 843-2241
lapwai.org

Significance: Where Lillian Marie Bounds Disney, Walt's wife, attended high school (Walt Disney Family Museum plaque).

LAPWAI

☐ **Lapwai Middle/High School**

ARRIVED
5 DEC 19??
WALT DISNE?

WALT'S PASSPORT

Chapter 39
Lewiston, Idaho

Living Room of Lillian's Brother

918 Third Street
Lewiston ID 83501
cityoflewiston.org

Significance: The location of Walt and Lillian's wedding.

Walt and Lillian Disney were married here on July 13, 1925. Since Lillian's father was deceased, her brother, chief of the Lewiston Fire Department, gave her away. They were married by Rev. Somerville (Walt's Apartment, July 13, 2013). She wore a dress which she had made herself. Walt paid $75 for Lillian's ring (Thomas, 1994; Walt's Apartment, July 13, 2013). "After the wedding, the bride and groom boarded a westbound train to connect with the *H.E. Alexander*, a coastwise steamer. They planned to take it from Seattle to Los Angeles. On their wedding night, Walt developed an infected tooth" (Miller, 1956, p. 89).

Where Lillian attended business college for 2 years after graduating from high school (Walt Disney Family Museum plaque).

Where Lillian's father, Willard, died
(Walt Disney Family Museum plaque).

While in Lewiston, visit the Nez Perce County Historical Society, Inc. & Museum: nezpercecountymuseum.com

LEWISTON

ARRIVED
5 DEC 1901
WALT DISN

☐ **918 Third Street**

WALT'S PASSPORT

Chapter 40
Spalding, Idaho

Specific location unknown.

Significance: Where Lillian Disney, Walt's wife, was born.
(Source: Walt Disney Family Museum plaque)

ILLINOIS

Chicago W

Food Available

Guided
Tour Available

Not Open to
the Public

Original Structure
Gone

Train
Connection

Parking
Fee

Post Death
Tribute

Hotel

Must See

Multimedia

Admission
Fee

Drive By
Location

Chapter 41
Chicago, Illinois
The Birthplace of Walt Disney

Walt Lived Here: 1901 to 1906 and 1917 to 1919
(except for his service in France)

December 5, 2013
"Walt Disney Day"
Declared by the Mayor of Chicago

The Walt Disney Birthplace

2156 North Tripp Avenue
(Original Address: 1249 Tripp Avenue)
Chicago IL 60639
(323) 663-7878
thewaltdisneybirthplace.org
cecciwdb.org

Significance: Walt is believed to have
been born on the second floor of this
home in the Hermosa neighborhood
on December 5, 1901. Back in the late 1800s, this area was
known as Northwesttown
(Thomas, 1998).

The birth home is now owned by Dina
Benadon and Brent Young of California. It is expected to open as
The Center for Early Childhood Creativity and Innovation
(cecciwdb.org).

There are brown honorary street signs that read: "Disney Family Avenue."

HISTORY OF THE HOME

"Elias (Walt's father) purchased property on the southwest corner of Tripp Avenue on October 31, 1891. On November 23, 1892, Elias obtained a permit to build a two-story, 18 x 28 foot wood cottage for $800. Flora, Elias' wife, drew up the architectural plans and Elias built the house. In early 1893, the Disney family settled into their new home with their two sons: Herbert and Raymond. Shortly thereafter, their third son, Roy, was born on June 24, 1893. Walter Elias Disney was born on December 5, 1901, on the second floor. And on December 6, 1903, the Disneys welcomed their fifth child, Ruth. On February 10, 1906, Elias sold the property to Walter Chamberlain, moving his family to Marceline, Missouri" (Walt Disney Birthplace, n.d., n.p.).

"In 1991, Chicago attempted to designate the property as a historical landmark but the owner fought the designation and won, putting the home at risk of demolition" (Walt Disney Birthplace, n.d., n.p.).

On March 3, 2016, The Walt Disney Company pledged $250,000 to support the Center for Early Childhood Creativity and Innovation (D23 Disney Fan Club, March 7, 2016). Disney CEO Bob Iger said that day: "Chicago holds a special place in the history of The Walt Disney Company. The Disney story actually started here...in a house on Tripp Avenue, where Walt Disney was born. The house is still standing at the corner of Tripp and Palmer in Hermosa, and it means a lot to us to see the effort to restore it back to its original condition....and to hear that it will one day be a children's creativity center, inspiring future generations of young dreamers and innovators" (Walt Disney Birthplace, March 3, 2016, n.p.).

"The Center for Early Childhood Creativity and Innovation (CECCI) will encourage children of all ages, abilities and experiences to imagine, create and embrace innovative thinking. CECCI is also restoring the famed Walt Disney Birthplace in the Hermosa Neighborhood of Chicago to serve as a source of inspiration for the next generation of creative thinkers. The 1,200 square foot house will become much more than an arts center or a museum. It will be an experiential learning site that inspires creativity, and it will deliver this uplifting message: if Walt Disney could rise from such humble beginnings to become one of our greatest visionaries, then true creative genius can come from anywhere, at any time. It will inspire future generations in ways we can only begin to imagine" (CECCI, n.d., n.p.).

In 2016, the first "Creativity Days" were held at this site. And in that same year, the "Creativi-TREE" was planted in front of the home. That tree is "a living, ever-growing celebration of the hopes and dreams of all children who come to the Disney home" (Walt Disney Birthplace, May 10, 2016, n.p.).

St. Paul Congregational Church

(now Iglesia Evangelica Bautista Betania: Bethany Evangelical Baptist Church)
2255 North Keeler Avenue
Chicago IL 60639

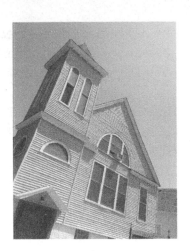

Significance: Where Walt was baptized.

Walt Disney was named after Walter Parr, the pastor of the church. Elias Disney helped build the church. The church building was dedicated on October 14, 1900 (Elias Disney, n.d.).

Disney Family Home

(no longer in existence)
1523 West Ogden Avenue
Chicago IL 60526

Significance: When Walt's family returned to Chicago in 1917, they lived here. However, the original home no longer exists. It has been replaced by commercial buildings.

McKinley High School

(now Chicago Bulls Prep High School)
2040 West Adams Street
Chicago IL 60611
(773) 534-7599
chicagobullscollegeprep.noblenetwork.org

Significance: Where Walt attended high school for one year, never graduating from high school.

Walt drew pictures for the school newspaper, *The Voice*, while at McKinley High School.

The school was named in honor of former U.S. President William McKinley.

Chicago Academy of Fine Arts

(now defunct)
81 East Monroe Street
Chicago IL 60603

Significance: In 1917 and 1918, Walt took night courses at the Chicago Academy of Fine Arts under the direction of artist and educator Louis Grell (Louis Grell Foundation, September 21, 2013). These were cartoon correspondence courses that Walt took three nights a week (Miller, 1956).

This was a private art school run by Carl Wertz (Miller, 1956).

"The Chicago Academy of Fine Arts is now defunct, and the building has been gone since the 38-story Willoughby Tower replaced the older 8-story Willoughby Building in 1929" (Weiss, 2008, n.p.).

Wilson Station: 'L' Metro System

4620 North Broadway
Chicago IL 60640
(888) 968-7282
transitchicago.com/travel_information/station.aspx?StopId=140

Significance: Walt worked as a "gate jerker" at the Wilson Avenue elevated railroad line at 40 cents an hour (Warner, 2014). In 1948, Walt rode the "L" on a return visit (See Burnham Park on pages 190-191).

Wilson is a station on the Chicago Transit Authority's Red Line, part of the Chicago 'L' metro system and is located in the Uptown neighborhood of Chicago, Illinois.

"The 35th Street "L" (elevated train) station was destroyed in 1962 by fire. The Chicago Transit Authority (CTA) opened a new station at 35th Street in 1965. It's now called the 35-Bronzeville-IIT station on CTA Green Line" (Weiss, 2008, n.p.).

Post Office in the Federal Building

(now the Kluczynski Federal Building)
230 South Dearborn Street
Chicago IL 60604
(312) 353-4475
gsa.gov/portal/content/101886

Significance: Walt worked at the post office in the building from July until September 1918.

"The downtown post office in Chicago's old Federal Building was razed in 1965 to make way for the 45-floor Kluczynski Federal Building" (Weiss, 2008, n.p.).

O-Zell Factory

1301 West 15th Street
Chicago IL 60608

Formerly a jelly and juice company.

Significance: Elias bought into the company and worked there. Walt worked there for a very short period of time. Elias invested $16,000 (plus $20 from Walt) and served as Head of Plan Construction. In 1920, O-Zell went bankrupt (Thomas, 1994).

According to Diane Disney Miller (1956), Walt "nailed up boxes, mashed apples to make pectin for jelly, and ran the jar washer and the jar capper" (p. 35).

Burnham Park

5491 South Lake Shore Drive
Chicago IL 60615
(312) 742-5369
chicagoparkdistrict.com/parks/Burnham-Park

Significance: Site of the 1893 Columbian Exposition, where Walt's father, Elias worked. Walt returned here for the Chicago Railroad Fair in Burnham Park in 1948 with his animator friend Ward Kimball.

Walt and Ward traveled by Santa Fe Super Chief (Thomas, 1994). Walt and Ward were able to see a depiction of the Lincoln funeral train. "Walt's eyes filled with tears every time he saw the Lincoln train cross the stage" (Thomas, 1994, p. 214). According to Thomas, Walt and Ward spent all of their days and evenings at the show. "They climbed in and out of engine cabs, rode them across the stage during the show, talked endlessly to old-time engineers and firemen. When Walt returned home, he told Lilly, 'That was the most fun I ever had in my life'"
(Thomas, 1994, p. 214).

Walt also visited the Museum of Science and Industry and saw the 999 Steam Locomotive which was displayed at the 1893 World's Fair.

Ward Kimball stated:
"While in Chicago with Walt he asked if there were any places I wanted to go. I told him of a jazz place, and he said 'You can do that anytime! Let's go ride the El.' So we rode that elevated train half the night and he was looking out the window reliving his childhood" (JustDisney.com, 2017, n.p).

"Walt even got a chance to perform a bit part in one of the performances of 'Wheels A Rolling,' a pageant featuring a variety of scenes about how the railroads helped build America. Walt, in stovepipe hat and frock coat, pantomimed the role of a passenger disembarking a train and being served a meal by the famous Harvey Girls" (Korkis, September 10, 2014, n.p.).

Art Institute of Chicago

Thorne Miniature Rooms (Lower Level)
111 South Michigan Avenue
Chicago IL 60603-6404
(312) 443-3600
artic.edu/aic/collections/thorne

Significance: Walt collected miniatures as a hobby (Smith, 2006). Walt visited the Thorne Miniature Rooms in 1960. (Art Institute of Chicago facebook page and Walt Disney Family Museum photo caption).

"The 68 Thorne Miniature Rooms enable one to glimpse elements of European interiors from the late 13th century to the 1930s and American furnishings from the 17th century to the 1930s. Painstakingly constructed on a scale of one inch to one foot, these fascinating models were conceived by Mrs. James Ward Thorne of Chicago and constructed between 1932 and 1940 by master craftsmen according to her specifications" (Art Institute of Chicago, n.d, n.p).

 Download multiple apps:
artic.edu/visit/maps-guides-and-apps

Red Cross Automotive and Mechanical Bureau Department

4064 Cottage Grove Avenue
Chicago IL 60653

Significance: Walt Disney and Russell Maas (Walt's fellow postal worker) dropped off their American Red Cross applications at the one-story brick building, which was "used as a headquarters for Red Cross drivers who took part in a four-week training course at Camp Scott, before being posted overseas" (Lesjak, 2015, p. 31).

Camp Scott

Temporary Red Cross Training Facility
Cottage Grove neighborhood
Vicinity of East 60th Street between South Cottage Grove Avenue
        and South Drexel Avenue
Near the University of Chicago

Currently that space is a parking lot.

Significance: On September 25, 1918, Walt reported for duty here. He received his training at Forest Park (Lesjak, 2015). This was the Red Cross Motor Training School. Walt completed a four-week training course "that included an automotive repair class taught by local Yellow Cab mechanics, driver training, and military drill instruction" (Lesjak, 2015, p. 33).

While at camp, Walt was exposed to an influenza virus and sent home temporarily to recover (Lesjak, 2015). As a result, Walt was delayed one day in being sent to France (Lesjak, 2015).

Disney recollected on his time at Camp Scott:
"There was an amusement park...we [lived in] tents. [I] had to work under cars, in magnetos and things. They put us in trucks and put us in holes and we had to [drive] out of holes. [T]hey washed you up if you couldn't drive a car. If you couldn't make it...you were then made a helper" (Lesjak, 2015, p. 34).

Camp Scott is named after George E. Scott, who was the general manager of the American Red Cross in Washington, D.C. (Lesjak, 2015).

OTHER CHICAGO STOPS WITH DISNEY CONNECTIONS

Walt Disney Magnet School

4140 North Marine Drive
Chicago IL 60613
(773) 534-5840
disney.cps.edu

Significance: A school that bears Disney's name.

"It opened in the 1970's and was the first magnet school in the City of Chicago. Walt Disney Magnet School is an open spaced environment with a team teaching format. There are approximately 1600 students in preschool through eighth grades. Disney is part of the Fine Arts Magnet School Cluster and delivers arts and technology integrated instruction" (Walt Disney Magnet School, 2008, n.p.).

"In 2004, Diane Disney Miller (the daughter of Walt and Lillian Disney) helped dedicate a $250,000 animation lab that her family helped fund at this school" (Walt Disney Magnet School, 2008, n.p.).

Disney II Magnet School

Elementary School: Kedvale Campus

3815 North Kedvale Avenue

Chicago IL 60641

(773) 534-3750

disneyiimagnet.org

High School: Lawndale Campus

3900 North Lawndale

Chicago IL 60618

(773) 534-5010

 **Significance:** A school (in 2 locations) that bears Walt Disney's name.

"In 2007, due to its strong history of success, the Walt Disney Magnet School was invited to replicate by the Chicago Public Schools (CPS). After a rigorous and comprehensive application and review process, it was announced that Disney II would open as a new Chicago Public School and as a "replication" of CPS's Walt Disney Magnet School" (Disney II Magnet, n.d., n.p.).

William P. Nixon Elementary

2121 North Keeler Avenue

Chicago IL 60639

(773) 534-4375

nixon.cps.edu

Significance: Nixon Elementary is the school that Walt's older brothers Roy, Herbert, and Raymond Disney attended when the family was living in the home where Walt was born.

In June 1935 in Chicago, Walt lunched with his Kansas City childhood friend, Walt Pfeiffer (Madden, 2017). This was while Walt, Lillian, Roy, and Edna were bound to New York for their European vacation.

CHICAGO

- ☐ Red Cross Automotive & Mechanical Bureau Dept.
- ☐ Art Institute of Chicago
- ☐ Burnham Park
- ☐ Campus Scott
- ☐ Chicago Academy of Fine Arts
- ☐ Disney Family Home
- ☐ Disney II Magnet School
- ☐ McKinley High School
- ☐ O'Zell Factory site
- ☐ Post Office
- ☐ St. Paul Congregational Church
- ☐ Walt Disney Birthplace
- ☐ Walt Disney Magnet School
- ☐ William P. Nixon Elementary School
- ☐ Wilson Station

ARRIVED
5 DEC 1901
WALT DISNEY

WALT'S PASSPORT

IOWA

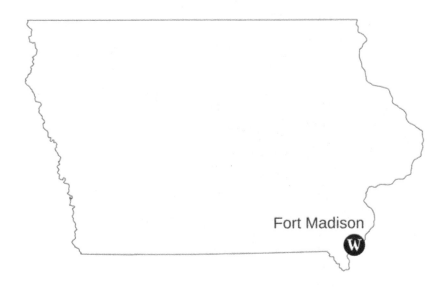

Fort Madison

 Food Available

 Guided Tour Available

 Not Open to the Public

 Original Structure Gone

 Train Connection

 Parking Fee

 Post Death Tribute

 Hotel

 Must See

 Multimedia

 Admission Fee

 Drive By Location

Chapter 42
Fort Madison, Iowa

Home of Flora Call Disney's Sister

Location of home is unknown.

Significance: In April 1906 (Walt was 4 years old), Walt and his family visited Flora's sister, Alice, in Fort Madison, Iowa while en route from Chicago to Marceline. Alice's husband was Mike Martin, who worked as an engineer on the Santa Fe Railway (Silvester, 2014).

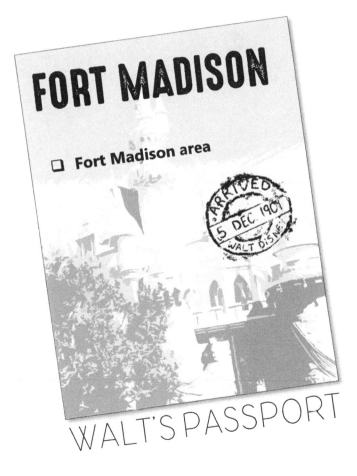

WALT'S PASSPORT

KANSAS

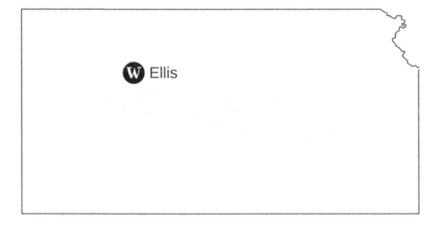

W Ellis

Food Available

Guided
Tour Available

Not Open to
the Public

Original Structure
Gone

Train
Connection

Parking
Fee

Post Death
Tribute

Hotel

Must See

Multimedia

Admission
Fee

Drive By
Location

Chapter 43
Ellis, Kansas
Located 4 Hours West of Kansas City

Mount Hope Cemetery
Old Highway 40
Ellis KS 67637

Significance: This is the town where Walt Disney's paternal grandparents (Kepple Elias Disney and Mary Richardson) are buried. Kepple died May 24, 1891. Mary died March 10, 1909. (Cruise, 2012).

Kepple Elias Disney is buried in Section 4, Lot 35, Space 1, according to Ellis city officials. Mary is buried next to Kepple, but there is no marker there (personal communication, S. Disney, June 20, 2017).

In 1878, Kepple and Mary and their nine children moved to Ellis (Cruise, 2012).

"Hearing of a gold strike in California, he [Kepple] set out in 1877 with eighteen-year-old Elias and his second-eldest son, Robert. They got only as far as Kansas when Kepple changed plans and purchased just over three hundred acres from the Union Pacific Railroad, which was trying to entice people to settle at division points along the train route it was laying through the state. (Since the Disneys were not American citizens, they could not acquire land under the Homestead Act.) The area in which the family settled, Ellis County in the northwestern quadrant of Kansas about halfway across the state, was frontier and rough" (Gabler, 2006).

"The winter of 1885-86 had been especially brutal in Ellis. Will Disney, Kepple's youngest son, remembered the snow drifting into ten-to-twelve-foot banks, forcing the settlers from the wagon trains heading west to camp in the schoolhouse for six weeks until the weather broke. The snow was so deep that the train tracks were cleared only when six engines were hitched to a dead locomotive with a snowplow and made run after run at the drifts, inching forward and backing up, gradually nudging through. Kepple, tired of the cruel Kansas weather, decided to join a neighbor family on a reconnaissance trip to Lake County, in the middle of Florida, where the neighbors had relatives. Elias went with him" (Gabler, 2006, p. 5).

According to Dave Smith (n.d.), Roy O. Disney traveled to Ellis in Fall 1912 to the home of his uncle, William Harvey Disney, to help with the harvest. Roy had carved his initials into a limestone block from a building on the farm.

 This Mount Hope Cemetery video references Kepple Elias Disney's grave. Search "Mount Hope Cemetery Tour, Ellis KS" on YouTube.

For more information about Ellis: ellis.ks.us

Ellis is also home to The Chrysler Boyhood Home & Museum. Walter P. Chrysler founded the Chrysler Corporation. chryslerboyhoodhome.com/index.asp

For more information on Elias Disney and Ellis, see pages 353-354.

ARRIVED
5 DEC 1901
WALT DISNE

ELLIS

☐ **Mount Hope Cemetery**

WALT'S PASSPORT

LOUISIANA

New Orleans

Food Available

Guided
Tour Available

Not Open to
the Public

Original Structure
Gone

Train
Connection

Parking
Fee

Post Death
Tribute

Hotel

Must See

Multimedia

Admission
Fee

Drive By
Location

Chapter 44
New Orleans, Louisiana

Significance: On November 22, 1963, Walt Disney and five Disney executives flew into New Orleans on a scouting trip for the site of Disney World (Thomas, 1994).

"Then he (Walt) ordered the pilot to New Orleans. As the Disney executives drove from the airport to their hotel, they noticed crowds of people huddled around radios and watching television sets in store windows. When Walt arrived at the hotel he learned what had happened: President Kennedy had been shot" (Thomas, 1994, p. 334). Hotel is unknown.

In reference to Club 33 at Disneyland:
(for more information on Club 33, see pages 32-33).
"In April 1966, Walt and Lillian Disney travelled to New Orleans with designer Emile Kuri, who had decorated the sets of *Mary Poppins* and *20,000 Leagues Under the Sea*, to select many of the beautiful antiques which would be featured in the club" (Glover, August 18, 2011, n.p.).

□ New Orleans area

WALT'S PASSPORT

MASSACHUSETTS

Cambridge W
Brookline W

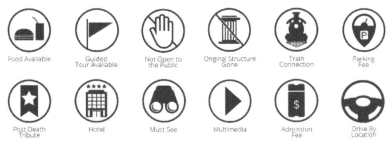

Food Available	Guided Tour Available	Not Open to the Public
Original Structure Gone	Train Connection	Parking Fee
Post Death Tribute	Hotel	Must See
Multimedia	Admission Fee	Drive By Location

Chapter 45
Brookline, Massachusetts

Brookline, Massachusetts
Greater Boston Area

Significance: "Walt and Lillian spent the night of June 22 in suburban Brookline, at the home of Dr. Roger I. Lee, an eminent Boston physician and a member of the Harvard Corporation, the university's governing body" (Barrier, 2015).

Location of Lee's house is unknown.

BROOKLINE

☐ **Brookline area**

ARRIVED 5 DEC. 1901 WALT DISNEY

WALT'S PASSPORT

Chapter 46
Cambridge, Massachusetts

Harvard University

Cambridge MA 02138
(617) 495-1000
harvard.edu

Walt visited here in 1938 and 1943 (Barrier, 2015).

Walter Elias Disney, A. M. Hon. '38

Significance: Walt received an honorary degree on June 23, 1938 from Harvard University, his third honorary degree (Barrier, 2015).

"Disney's honorary degree citation read: 'A magician who has created a modern dwelling for the Muses'" (Korkis, 2013, n.p.).

1943 VISIT
"Walt visited Harvard again almost five years later, after his studio had passed through tumult—a financial crisis, a traumatic strike—that he could hardly have envisioned in 1938. He arrived in New York on February 1, 1943, a Monday, and was planning to be in the East long enough to attend the Broadway premiere of *Saludos Amigos* on February 12. In between, he visited Cambridge for a couple of days. As the *Harvard Alumni Bulletin* reported in its issue of February 13, 1943:

Walter Elias Disney, A.M. Hon. '38, revisited Harvard last week to consult with Dr. Earnest A. Hooton, Professor of Anthropology and Chairman of the Department of Anthropology, on a forthcoming technicolor [sic] film ridiculing *Der Führer*'s ideas of

Aryan racial supremacy. Mr. Disney, accompanied by two of his studio script writers [Joe Grant and Dick Huemer], told the Boston press in an on-the-steps interview at the Faculty Club that he plans to leave Hitler 'out of the picture,' because he thinks that "too much attention has already been given to that guy" (Barrier, 2015, n.p.).

"While at Harvard, Mr. Disney inspected the Harvard Film Service, saw the Harvard reading films, and admired as an artist-craftsman the wonder of the glass flowers at the University Museum. He was greeted by professors and deans, and even by a small boy movie fan, whom he patted on the head" (Barrier, 2015, n.p.).

CAMBRIDGE

☐ Harvard University

ARRIVED 5 DEC 1937 WALT DISNEY

WALT'S PASSPORT

MICHIGAN

Hickory Corners

Battle Creek

Kalamazoo

Dearborn

Food Available

Guided Tour Available

Not Open to the Public

Original Structure Gone

Train Connection

Parking Fee

Post Death Tribute

Hotel

Must See

Multimedia

Admission Fee

Drive By Location

Chapter 47
Battle Creek, Michigan

Post Foods

275 Cliff Street
Battle Creek MI 49014
(269) 966-1000
postfoods.com

Significance: A major licensing agreement for Walt was with Postum Cereals.

"In 1934, Disney employee Kay Kamen signed a $1.5 million deal with the Postum Cereals Company of Battle Creek, Michigan (later General Foods), for the rights to print Mickey Mouse and other Disney character cut-outs on the back of Post Toasties cereal packages. The income gave a major boost to the studio. The cut-out concept was soon expanded to include cut-out-and-assemble toys, games, activities, and comic strips. The deal was renewed annually until 1942" (Video screen on Disney merchandising, Walt Disney Family Museum).

"In 2015, Post Foods purchased MOM Brands (formerly Malt-O-Meal Co.) creating the third largest breakfast cereal company in the U.S. The combined company is now called Post Consumer Brands and is headquartered in Lakeville, Minnesota" (Post Cereals, n.d., n.p.).

BATTLE CREEK

☐ **Post Foods**

ARRIVED
5 DEC 1901
WALT DISNEY

WALT'S PASSPORT

Chapter 48
Dearborn, Michigan

Greenfield Village

(Part of The Henry Ford)
20900 Oakwood Boulevard
Dearborn MI 48124-5029
(800) 835-5237
thehenryford.org/visit/greenfield-village

Significance: Walt visited The Henry Ford Museum/ Greenfield Village on these three dates:

April 12, 1940
August 20, 1943
August 23, 1948
(Ward Kimball accompanied Walt on the 1948 trip after visiting a railroad event in Chicago).

April 12, 1940 visit:
(From the *Greenfield Village Journal*)
"Walt Disney, creator of the world-famous movie character, Mickey Mouse, visited the Village and Museum today. He showed great interest in everything mechanical, examining engines and old autos closely. He had a good time with Mr. Tremear while posing for a tin-type. In the Museum Theater he spoke for a few moments to the school children. He was accompanied by Mrs. Disney, and by Ben Sharpsteen, his chief animator. Wm. B. Stout was his host" (PDF of the Journal provided by the Benson Ford Research Center, n.p.).

August 18, 1943 visit:

(From the *Village Journal*)

"Wednesday, August 18, Mrs. Walt Disney and her daughter, Diane, were among the visitors to the Village. Friday, accompanied by Mr. Disney, they went through the Museum. The Disneys found many things in both which interested them, and found their visit very enjoyable" (PDF of the Journal provided by the Benson Ford Research Center, n.p.).

August 23, 1948 visit:

"The duo [Walt and Ward Kimball] visited Henry Ford's Greenfield Village, which featured four centuries of historic buildings moved from their original locations and laid out in an old fashioned Main Street design" (Greenfield Village Visit, n.d., n.p.).

Benson Ford Research Center

(Part of The Henry Ford)
20900 Oakwood Boulevard
Dearborn MI 48124-5029
thehenryford.org/collections-and-research/services/
(313) 982-6020
research.center@thehenryford.org

Significance: This research center contains some photos of Walt Disney's visits to Greenfield Village and with Ford Motor Company officials. Walt designed the Ford Pavilion (among others) for the 1964-1965 World's Fair in New York City (see pages 282-284).

14 Digital Artifacts:

November 26, 1962 Photograph of Henry Ford II and Walt Disney
https://www.thehenryford.org/collections-and-research/digital-collections/artifact/78935

February 18, 1943 Letter from Walt Disney to the Ford Motor Company
https://www.thehenryford.org/collections-and-research/digital-collections/artifact/428034

1943 Seasons Greetings Card from Walt Disney and his Staff to Henry Ford
https://www.thehenryford.org/collections-and-research/digital-collections/artifact/341325#slide=gs-340927

April 12, 1940 Tintype Print of Walt Disney posting in the Greenfield Village Tintype Studio
https://www.thehenryford.org/collections-and-research/digital-collections/artifact/341259

November 26, 1962 Photographic Print of Henry Ford II and Walt Disney viewing the Ford Pavilion Model
https://www.thehenryford.org/collections-and-research/digital-collections/artifact/67807

August 23, 1948 Tintype Print of Walt Disney and Ward Kimball posting in the Greenfield Village Tintype Studio
https://www.thehenryford.org/collections-and-research/digital-collections/artifact/341261

August 20, 1943 Photograph print of Walt Disney and Daughter Visiting the Henry Ford Museum
https://www.thehenryford.org/collections-and-research/digital-collections/artifact/389753

August 20, 1943 Photograph print of Walt Disney and Family Visiting the Henry Ford Museum
https://www.thehenryford.org/collections-and-research/digital-collections/artifact/427104#slide=gs-379926

1964 Photograph Print of Walt Disney and Robert Lamerson Inspecting the Ford Motor Company Pavilion for the 1964 New York World's Fair
https://www.thehenryford.org/collections-and-research/digital-collections/artifact/2220

August 20, 1943 Photograph Prints of Walt Disney Visiting the Henry Ford Museum
https://www.thehenryford.org/collections-and-research/digital-collections/artifact/427110
https://www.thehenryford.org/collections-and-research/digital-collections/artifact/427069
https://www.thehenryford.org/collections-and-research/digital-collections/artifact/427094

1964-1965 Brochure Promoting the Ford Pavilion:
"Ride Walt Disney's Magic Skyway"
https://www.thehenryford.org/collections-and-research/digital-collections/artifact/386505#slide=gs-292831

The Edison Institute Guest Register: July 1943-April 1944
Walt's signature and his daughter, Diane Disney's signatures appear in this book:
https://www.thehenryford.org/collections-and-research/digital-collections/artifact/427522#slide=gs-379934

Through special request of the Benson Ford Research Center, the originals of these documents can be viewed.

Henry Ford Museum of American Innovation™

(Part of The Henry Ford)
20900 Oakwood Boulevard
Dearborn MI 48124-5029
(800) 835-5237
thehenryford.org/visit/henry-ford-museum/

Significance: Here there are several Walt Disney related artifacts/exhibits on display.

DRIVING AMERICA EXHIBIT
In the "Wish You Were Here" display case, there is a Disneyland Souvenir Booklet featuring a photo of Walt with the schematic drawing of Disneyland.

YOUR PLACE IN TIME EXHIBIT
Outside of this exhibit is an image of *Snow White and the Seven Dwarfs*. In addition, the Hollywood Souvenir Store display case has a few items from *Pinocchio*. The timeline references the 1955 opening of Disneyland.

Ford Rouge Factory/Plant

20900 Oakwood Boulevard
Dearborn MI 48124-5029
(800) 835-5237
thehenryford.org/visit/ford-rouge-factory-tour

Significance: Walt Disney visited here in April 1940.

Tours of the factory are available:
thehenryford.org/visit/ford-rouge-factory-tour/highlights

"I have wanted to see the Ford plant for a long time. To me, the main point of interest was the assembly line. There is a strong similarity between the Ford assembly line and our animated picture business. We have hundreds of workers all helping to assemble the cartoon that you see in continuity. Of course, it's somewhat different to run an assembly line with temperamental artists" – Walt Disney speaking to a *Detroit Free Press* reporter on April 12, 1940, after a visit to Ford's Rouge plant in Dearborn. (Korkis, 2016, p. 83).

Note:
Walt Disney Imagineer Bob Gurr worked for Ford Motor Company and lived in Dearborn in 1952. According to Gurr, he lived on Haigh Street in Dearborn (personal communication, July 2015). Gurr was named a Disney Legend in 2004 (Smith, 2006).

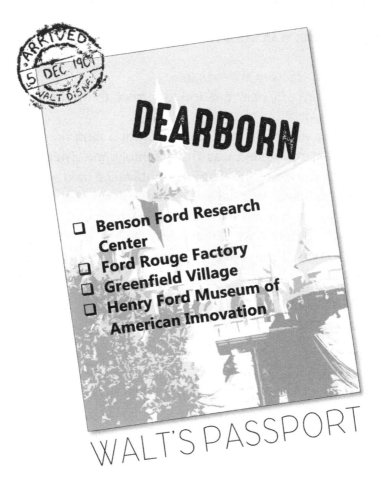

ARRIVED
15 DEC 1901
WALT DISNE

DEARBORN

- ☐ **Benson Ford Research Center**
- ☐ **Ford Rouge Factory**
- ☐ **Greenfield Village**
- ☐ **Henry Ford Museum of American Innovation**

WALT'S PASSPORT

Chapter 49
Hickory Corners, Michigan

Gilmore Car Museum

6865 West Hickory Road
Hickory Corners MI 49060
(269) 671-5089
gilmorecarmuseum.org

This exhibit is open seasonally,
April to November.

Significance: This museum contains several Disney artifacts. A 1930 Rolls-Royce Sedanca Deville used in the 1967 Walt Disney movie, *The Gnome-Mobile* was purchased by Mr. Donald Gilmore, the originator of the museum and is currently stored at the museum. The second Disney artifact is the movie set of the car's backseat, which Walt Disney personally gave to Gilmore because they were close friends. The oversized movie set is nearly four times larger than the rear seat of that 1930 Rolls Royce. It was installed and dedicated in the museum in September 1966, just three months before Walt Disney's death (Liberty, 2014).

The Gilmore Car Museum Research Library and Archival Facility, located in the Automotive Heritage Center, contains a variety of original photographs of Walt Disney from this visit with Donald Gilmore. In addition, there are several original letters sent by Walt Disney to Donald Gilmore.

According to the Gilmore Car Museum website, "Walt Disney visited the Gilmore Family and Donald's car collection on September 18, 1964, just two years before Donald would open his collection to the public. He signed Donald's guest book and listed his address as 'Disneyland U.S.A.'" (Gilmore Car Museum, 2016, n.p.).

About the Disney-Gilmore Connection:
"Walt Disney and Donald Gilmore were friends and neighbors in the Smoke Tree Ranch of Palm Springs, Calif. Gilmore, who became Upjohn president in 1944, was an original sponsor of Disneyland in Anaheim, Calif. An Upjohn Pharmacy was part of Main Street, U.S.A., when the [theme] park opened in 1955. Disney made multiple visits to Kalamazoo to spend time with Gilmore, including in 1964 when he also met with local children. Disney sold the Rolls-Royce to Gilmore for the cost of having it shipped to Hickory Corners. The set piece was installed and dedicated in the museum in September, 1966. Disney died on Dec. 15, 1966" (Liberty, 2014, n.p.).

For more information on Smoke Tree Ranch, see pages 101-103.

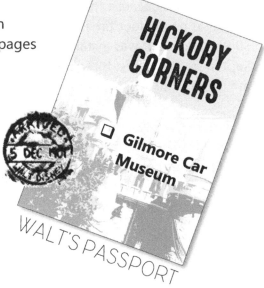

Chapter 50
Kalamazoo, Michigan

Kalamazoo Art Center

(now the Kalamazoo Institute of Arts (KIA))
314 South Park Street
Kalamazoo MI 49007
(269) 349-7775
kiarts.org

Significance: Walt Disney visited here in September 17-20, 1964 while visiting Mr. and Mrs. Donald Gilmore, on his way back from Washington, D.C. (*Kalamazoo Gazette* photo caption, n.d.; Korkis, May 11, 2016).

"The Gilmores made a deal with Walt Disney; they would donate money to the Chouinard Art Institute (see pages 75-76) if Disney donated money to the Kalamazoo Art Center. A dinner was arranged at the Kalamazoo Art Center for top donors to see Walt Disney as a guest speaker. Mr. [Alfred P.] Maurice and Walt Disney shared common interests and later spent an afternoon at the Kalamazoo Mall where Disney drew Mickey Mouse caricatures for children. Mr. Maurice later described Walt Disney as fascinating and child-like" (Kalamazoo Art Center, n.d., p. 2).

In 1966, the Walt Disney Children's Scholarship Fund was established as a memorial to Disney at the Gilmore Art Center. According to KIA representatives, that scholarship no longer exists (*Kalamazoo Gazette* photo caption, December 26, 1966; personal communication, B. Tate, July 20, 2015).

According to the KIA Executive Director, a Walt Disney Fund enabled the KIA to purchase several Asian pieces of art in the 1960s (personal communication, B. Tate, July 20, 2015).

About the Kalamazoo Art Center
"Donald and Genevieve Gilmore (of the Upjohn Pharmaceutical Company) were great advocates for the arts; Mr. Gilmore in music and Mrs. Gilmore the visual arts. The Gilmore family wanted to establish a community art program in honor of their deceased oldest daughter who was interested in art. They sought out Mr. [Alfred P.] Maurice and invited him to move to Kalamazoo to direct building of the community art program and center that would serve the entire community of Kalamazoo. The art building was designed to accommodate art exhibitions and education for the creative arts. The building included studio and office space and was intended to encourage productivity for faculty and students alike" (Kalamazoo Art Center, n.d., p. 1).

Upjohn Company

(now Pfizer Global Supply)
7000 Portage Road
Kalamazoo MI 49001-0199

Significance: Walt Disney visited here in September 1964 while visiting Mr. and Mrs. Donald Gilmore (*Kalamazoo Gazette photo caption, n.d.*).

'When Walt arrived, he wore on his suit lapel a flicker souvenir button from Disneyland. One image showed the face of Goofy while the other the phrase 'I'm Goofy About Disneyland.' He pinned extras on the VIPs who accompanied him on a tour of the Upjohn plant on that first day. He enjoyed a meal with them at the commissary..." (Korkis, May 11, 2016, n.p.).
Donald Gilmore was friends with Walt Disney and they were neighbors at Smoke Tree Ranch in Palm Springs, California (see pages 101-103 to read about Smoke Tree Ranch.)

Donald Gilmore was chairman of the board and managing director of The Upjohn Company and was one of the first sponsors of Disneyland (Korkis, May 11, 2016). Gilmore paid to have an Upjohn Pharmacy on Main Street, U.S.A. in Disneyland. That pharmacy was there from 1995 to 1971. Upjohn initially paid $29,000 to have this pharmacy in Disneyland (Korkis, May 11, 2016). However, annual costs were about $37,720 (Korkis, May 11, 2016).

"The front half of the store had a reproduction of an old-time apothecary shop based on three New York pharmacies that were in existence before 1886. In the back was a contemporary display with four revolving photo columns showing phases of present-day manufacturing, as well as a large aerial photo, on a nearby wall, of its Portage plant with descriptive captions" (Korkis, May 11, 2016, n.p.).

To learn more, visit:
mouseplanet.com/11400/The_Story_of_the_Upjohn_Pharmacy_at_Disneyland

---

Louie's News Agency and Pipe Shop
242 South Burdick (Address Back in 1964)
242 South Kalamazoo Mall (Today's Address)
Kalamazoo MI 49007

Significance: Walt Disney visited here on September 18, 1964 while visiting Mr. and Mrs. Donald Gilmore (*Kalamazoo Gazette* photo caption, n.d.). According to the *Kalamazoo Gazette*, Walt purchased some cigars here.

The nearest current business near where Louie's once was is Rustica restaurant, which is located at 236 South Kalamazoo Mall, Kalamazoo, MI 49007 (personal communication, S. Carlson, June 15, 2017).

Kalamazoo Mall

Located in Downtown Kalamazoo
Runs from North & South from Eleanor Street to
        West Lovell Street
S. and N. Kalamazoo Mall
Kalamazoo MI 49007
downtownkalamazoo.org/Visit/Districts/Kalamazoo-Mall.aspx

Significance: Walt Disney visited here on September 18, 1964 while visiting Mr. and Mrs. Donald Gilmore (*Kalamazoo Gazette photo caption, n.d.*).

Photo credit: MLive Media Group/Kalamazoo Gazette, ©1964 by Jerry Campbell, Used with written permission

Walt rode in the front seat of a tram belonging to the Downtown Kalamazoo Association on September 18, 1964. According to the *Kalamazoo Gazette*, Walt also strolled the Kalamazoo Mall.

The Kalamazoo Mall was the first outdoor pedestrian shopping mall in the United States (Living in Kalamazoo, n.d.).

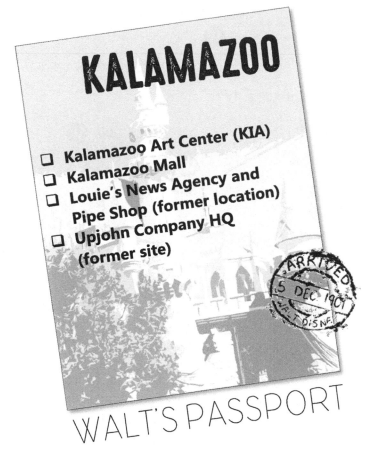

KALAMAZOO

- ☐ Kalamazoo Art Center (KIA)
- ☐ Kalamazoo Mall
- ☐ Louie's News Agency and Pipe Shop (former location)
- ☐ Upjohn Company HQ (former site)

ARRIVED
5 DEC 1901
WALT DISNE

WALT'S PASSPORT

MISSOURI

Marceline
W

W Kansas City

St. Louis **W**

W
Jefferson City

"I feel that my roots are in the great state of Missouri and that
I am a Missourian in every sense of the word,
even to the 'Show Me' tradition," stated Walt Disney
(Burnes, Butler & Viets, 2002, p. 141).

Food Available · Guided Tour Available · Not Open to the Public · Original Structure Gone · Train Connection · Parking Fee

Post Death Tribute · Hotel · Must See · Multimedia · Admission Fee · Drive By Location

Chapter 51
Jefferson City, Missouri

State of Missouri Capitol:
Hall of Famous Missourians

201 West Capitol Avenue
Jefferson City MO 65101
(573) 751-3339
house.mo.gov/content.aspx?info=/info/captour.htm

Free Admission

Significance: Walt was honored with a bust in 1993.

On May 12, 1993, Walt Disney was inducted into the Hall of Famous Missourians. There is a bust of Walt in the Missouri Capitol Building. He is 1 of 46 individuals in this Hall of Fame. Created by the Missouri Capitol Society, Inc., the Hall of Famous Missourians occupies the third floor rotunda area of the Capitol (Hall of Famous Missourians, n.d.).

Ron and Diane Miller (and a grandson) attended the opening representing the Disney family, and Dave Smith attended representing The Walt Disney Company (personal communication, D. Smith, July 5, 2017).

In 1917, Walt's first trip in his summer job as a news butcher for the Van Noy Interstate News Company was an eight hour trip from Kansas City to Jefferson City (Thomas, 1994). Walt stayed overnight and returned to Kansas City the next day (Miller, 1956).

JEFFERSON CITY

☐ **Hall of Famous Missourians**

ARRIVED
5 DEC. 1901
WALT DISN

WALT'S PASSPORT

228

Chapter 52
Kansas City, Missouri

Compilation of information assisted by Carly Dauer

Walt Lived Here: 1910 to 1917 and 1919 to 1923

33 Sites in Kansas City to explore

 MUST SEE
Disney Family Home
Kansas City Public Library
Kirk Building
Laugh-O-gram
Union Station

For a map of some of these sites, visit: thankyouwaltdisney.org

Benton Grammar School
Corner of 30th and Benton
Kansas City MO 64128

Significance: A place where Walt went to school.

The school is no longer there. It is the site of an apartment complex.

Walt and his sister Ruth attended grade school here from September 1911 through June 1917. Walt's claim to fame in this school was that the principal would take him from classroom to classroom every year to recite the Gettysburg Address (Thomas, 1994). Walt was a "voracious reader of Stevenson, Scott, Twain and Dickens" (Burnes, Butler & Viets, 2002, p. 56), but only an average student academically. Walt participated in the school track team, earning a medal in a relay (Burnes, Butler & Viets, 2002). Walt graduated from Benton on June 8, 1917 (Thomas, 1994).

Walt returned to Benton's homecoming and reunion on February 14, 1942 with 800 fellow former students. Walt formally presented murals of Disney characters (Burnes, Butler & Viets, 2002).

Bert Hudson's Barbershop

322 Westport Road
Kansas City MO 64111

Significance: Walt drew caricatures which were displayed in this shop.

"(Walt) developed an ease for caricature, and one day he drew impressions of the patrons at Bert Hudson's barbershop. The barber liked them so much he asked Walt to draw a new caricature every week. His work was framed on the barbershop wall, and Hudson cut Walt's hair for nothing" (Thomas, 1994, p. 37).

DeMolay International

10200 North Ambassador Drive
Kansas City MO 64153
(800) DEMOLAY
demolay.org

Significance: Walt joined and became a member in May 1920 (Walt Disney Family Museum photo caption).

"DeMolay is the premier youth leadership organization building young men of character and dedicated to making young men better people and leaders" (What is DeMolay?, 2017, n.p.).

"Walt joined in 1920 as the 107th member of the original Mother Chapter of DeMolay in Kansas City, Missouri barely a year after its formation in 1919 by Frank S. Land. Walt was 18 years old.

Walt received the DeMolay Legion of Honor in October 1931 a degree corresponding to that of a 33rd degree in Masonry, the highest attainable.

At the ceremony, Walt said, "I am proud to receive the Legion of Honor, but I feel as though I haven't done anything to merit it."

In 1936, Walt appeared as an honored guest at the first DeMolay Founder's Conference in Kansas City and to participate in the installation of 100 new members in the Legion of Honor of the Order of DeMolay.

Walt's involvement with DeMolay meant a great deal to him and he proudly wore a DeMolay ring on his right hand until the around 1948, when it was replaced by the Claddagh ring that both he and his wife wore for the rest of their lives.

 Disney was a member of the first class to be inducted (posthumously) into the DeMolay Hall of Fame on November 13, 1986" (Korkis, September 20, 2017, n.p.).

For Walt's profile in the DeMolay Hall of Fame: demolay.org/halloffame/bio.php?id=17

Disney Family Home (first)

2706 East 31st Street
Kansas City MO 64128

Significance: A place where Walt lived.

The Disney family, upon moving from Marceline to Kansas City, first rented a home in Spring 1911 (Burnes, Butler & Viets, 2002). This home was in the southern boundary of the *Kansas City Star* delivery route that Walt worked for his father, Elias (Burnes, Butler & Viets, 2002). (See page 233 for the paper route).

Disney Family Home

3028 Bellefontaine Avenue
Kansas City MO 64128

Significance: Walt lived here from 1910 to 1917 and 1919 to 1921 (Thomas, 1994).

Home is privately owned; be respectful to the occupants.

The garage behind the house is where "Walt conducted his first experiments in animation," according to Burnes, Butler, and Viets (2002, p. 49). A couple of doors down (3022 Bellefontaine) from this house was the Pfeiffer family and Walt befriended Walt Pfeiffer (Burnes, Butler & Viets, 2002).

Disney Family Paper Route: Route No. 145

 Significance: One of Walt's early jobs.

This paper route was assumed by the Disney family on July 1, 1911 (Burnes, Butler & Viets, 2002). There were 600-700 subscribers each for the various editions.

This paper route ran between 27th Street and 31st Street and Prospect Avenue and Indiana Street (Thankyouwaltdisney.org, n.d.). While Elias was in charge, the owner of the route on paper was R.O. Disney (Roy) (Burnes, Butler & Viets, 2002). Walt and Roy were required to assist Elias in the delivery of the *Kansas City Star* newspapers. According to Burnes, Butler and Viets (2002), "Walt and Roy were expected to carry each paper up the customers walk and, if possible, place it between the screen door and the front door. The papers couldn't be rolled or folded" (p. 50).

"At the age of 9, Walt found himself being pulled from his bed every morning well before dawn. Even before he got his breakfast he was expected to haul up to 25 to 30 pounds of newsprint through the neighborhood" (Burnes, Butler & Viets, 2002, p. 52).

Elias kept the income from the paper route, indicating to Walt and Roy that "they were working for their room and board" (Burnes, Butler & Viets, 2002, p. 50).

The family sold the route on March 17, 1917 (Burnes, Butler & Viets, 2002).

Electric Park

46th Street and the Paseo
Kansas City MO 64110

Significance: Provided inspiration for elements in Disneyland.

At the age of 9, Walt and his sister Ruth visited the second Electric Park, which was 15 blocks from their house (Burnes, Butler & Viets, 2002). It has been said that Walt incorporated the idea of a ring-road train and closing daily fireworks into Disneyland (Burnes, Butler & Viets, 2002).

Elsmere Hotel

1105 Linwood Boulevard
Kansas City MO 64190

Significance: In the fall of 1921, Walt formed a small business with a friend from work (Fred Harman) called Harman-Disney Studio. After working at the Film Ad Company all day, Walt would then head to work at the Harman-Disney Studio. "Sometimes it got so late that Walt wouldn't go home to sleep but instead crashed at the Elsmere Hotel" (Silvester, 2014, p. 82).

Forest Inn Cafe

McConahy Building
1127 East 31st Street
Kansas City MO 64109

Significance: A place where Walt enjoyed meals, often on credit.

The café was located on the first floor of the McConahy Building, where Walt's Laugh-O-gram Films was located. See pages 242-243 about Laugh-O-gram.

Gray Advertising Building

408 East 14th Street
Kansas City MO 64106

Significance: One of the places where Walt worked.

Here, in 1919, Walt worked for Pesmen & Rubin commercial art studio "doing advertising layouts and letterheads for... agricultural supply companies" (Burnes, Butler & Viets, 2002, p. 74). Walt made $50 a month (Burnes, Butler & Viets, 2002). Here was where Walt also met Ub Iwwerks (later shortened to Iwerks) (Burnes, Butler & Viets, 2002). Walt began working on the Newman Theatre account, for which he designed programs (Burnes, Butler & Viets, 2002). Walt's work here only lasted six weeks as it was only a seasonal position (Burnes, Butler & Viets, 2002).

Hallmark Visitors Center

2450 Grand Boulevard
Kansas City MO 64108
(816) 274-3613
hallmarkvisitorscenter.com

Admission is Free

Significance: Showcases one of Walt's early licensing partnerships.

In the Visitors Center, there are a couple of exhibits acknowledging that Hallmark was one of the first licensees for Walt Disney. The exhibit is located near the entrance to the Visitors Center.

"In 1931 Hall Brothers Company (later Hallmark Greeting Cards and then Hallmark, Inc.) signed a licensing agreement with Walt Disney to produce greeting cards of all kinds. This relationship flourished for 24 years" (Anderson, 2010, n.p.).

According to the Hallmark Visitors Center:
"In 1931, Hallmark founder J.C. Hall met with Walt Disney and struck an agreement for using the animator's well-loved characters on greeting cards and other products. Mickey Mouse made his debut on a Hallmark card one year later. From there, the men's partnership flourished and grew into a lasting friendship" (Hallmark Visitors Center, 2017).

Joyce Hall wrote a November 25, 1931 letter to Walt Disney expressing interest in a partnership (Regan, 2009). According to Regan (2009), Elizabeth Dilday Hall, wife of the founder and chairman of Hallmark Cards, Inc., attended the same grade school (Benton Grammar School) as Walt Disney.

When J.C. Hall was developing the Signboard Hill area of Kansas City, Walt served as a consultant on the project (Emerson, 2010).

Hotel Continental

Now known as Mark Twain Tower
106 West 11th Street
Kansas City MO 64105

Significance: Location of one of Walt's many lifetime honors.

On October 9, 1966 (two months before his death), Walt traveled to Kansas City to be honored at a national meeting of People to People (Burnes, Butler & Viets, 2002). "Disney was honored for his service on behalf of the People to People program and for advancing the cause of international understanding and friendship through motion pictures and television" (Burnes, Butler & Viets, 2002, p. 174). Disney was introduced by President Dwight D. Eisenhower (Burnes, Butler & Viets, 2002).

Isis Theatre

3102 Troost Avenue
Kansas City MO 64109

Significance: The Isis Theatre was considered the finest suburban theatre in Kansas City in the 1920s. It also happened to be located one block away from Laugh-O-gram Films (Salley, n.d.).

Walt partnered with the owners of the Isis Theatre to create commercials for the theatre. These were played to music on the organ by Carl Stalling, the musical director. The two also worked together on a series of song films that portrayed the lyrics of the songs while Stalling played them. Laugh-O-gram Films took part in a South Central Business Association parade in October of

1922. Disney and a few of his employees shot footage of the parade from a car with a sign saying the footage was to be shown the next day at the Isis Theatre (Salley, n.d.).

Kansas City Art Institute (KCAI)

Original Location/Name Where Walt Attended:
Fine Arts Institute of Kansas City
1021 McGee Street
Kansas City MO 64106

Significance: Part of Walt's formal art training.

Walt enjoyed Saturday classes at KCAI, which were held at the local YWCA (Burnes, Butler & Viets, 2002). According to KCAI (n.d.), Walt attended classes from 1915 to 1917.

Walt "had drawn only from plaster casts of famous pieces of sculpture...he loved being at a drawing board. He hated to leave it so much that if he had to go to the bathroom he'd put it off until the class was dismissed" (Miller, 1956, p. 36).

In May 1963, Walt returned to KCAI to receive a Distinguished Alumnus Award at an event at the Kansas City Country Club (Burnes, Butler & Viets, 2002). "The award cited Disney for his significant contributions to the art of visual communications" (Burnes, Butler & Viets, 2002, p. 174).

Current Location:
4415 South Warwick
      Boulevard
Kansas City MO 64111
(800) 522-5224
kcai.edu

Nothing at either location currently associated with or acknowledges Walt Disney. The KCAI website does acknowledge that Walt Disney was previous student.

Kansas City International Airport (MCI)

Kansas City MO 64153

flykci.com/parking/parking-lots-and-maps

Significance: At the B-7 Bus Stop in the economy parking lot at the airport, there is a kiosk entitled, "Mouse Tale" that pays tribute to Walt Disney as a previous resident of Kansas City.

Photo by Peter Whitehead

Kansas City Public Library

Where Walt Visited:

(Now home to Ozark National Life Insurance Co.)
9th and Locust
Kansas City MO 64106

Current Location (Central Library):

14 West 10th Street
Kansas City MO 64105
(816) 701-3400
kclibrary.org/library-locations/central-library

Significance: Where Walt learned part of his camera training.

Walt and Ub Iwerks checked out books here:

E.G. Lutz's
*Animated Cartoons: How They Are Made,
Their Origin and Development*

Eadweard Muybridge's *Animals in Motion*

"Everyone has been remarkably influenced by a book, or books.
In my case it was a book on cartoon animation. I discovered it in
the Kansas City library at the time I was preparing to make
motion picture animation my life's work. The book told me all
that I need to know as a beginner...Finding that book was one of
the most important and useful events in my life," stated Walt
(Smith, 1994, p. 15).

Both books are available in the reference section, but cannot be
checked out. These are replicas of the books that Walt reviewed.

Kansas City Slide Co./Kansas City Film Ad Co.

(Now The Kirk Building)
1332 Grand Avenue
1015 Central Street (Plaque)
2449 Charlotte
Kansas City MO 64105

THE KIRK BUILDING

1015 Central was built in 1908 and expanded in 1925. It was here in 1920 that Walt Disney was introduced to the basics of motion picture production and animation while working for The Kansas City Slide Company. In 1983, when much of the neighborhood was in decline, Phil Kirk purchased and renovated this venerable structure. This project was his first of many major contributions to Downtown revitalization. Under Kirk's leadership DST Realty completed the historic restoration and new construction of 38 buildings on Downtown's west side. With Phil Kirk's support Crossroads Academy of Kansas City opened on this site in 2012 fulfilling a long-held dream for an academically rigorous school in the heart of revitalized Downtown Kansas City, Missouri.

Significance: One of the places where Walt worked.

This company had at least three locations. Walt worked at the office on Central Street. That building is now known as "The Kirk Building." On the side of the building, there is a plaque that mentions Walt Disney: "It was here in 1920 that Walt Disney was introduced to the basics of motion picture production and animation while working for The Kansas City Slide Company."

Walt was one of 16 staff members and his initial pay of $40/month increased to $60/month (Burnes, Butler & Viets, 2002).

Kaycee Studios

FIRST LOCATION

(Streetcar Barn)
30th and Holmes
Kansas City MO 64109

Significance: One of Walt's many early studios.

This first location was established in Fall 1921 with Walt's friend, Fred Harman (Susanin, 2011). According to Susanin (2011), Walt and Fred rented this space secretly.

SECOND LOCATION
(Peiser Building)
3239 Troost Avenue
Kansas City MO 64109

Significance: One of Walt's many early studios.

These studios, named Kaycee (for Kansas City: KC), were the studios prior to the establishment of Laugh-O-gram Films.

Laugh-O-gram Films
McConahy Building
1127 East 31st Street
Kansas City MO 64109
thankyouwaltdisney.org

Significance: One of Walt's many early studios – his most significant one to this point in his life.

Laugh-O-gram Films was established by Walt in May 1922 (Susanin, 2011). Walt had raised $15,000 to start this studio (Burnes, Butler & Viets, 2002). The phone number had a Hyde Park exchange: HY-6309 (Burnes, Butler & Viets, 2002). The studio was on the second floor; just below it was the Forest Inn Café (Burnes, Butler & Viets, 2002). The original team numbered 15 employees (Burnes, Butler & Viets, 2002).

Between April and November of 1922, five fairy tale cartoons were created (Burnes, Butler & Viets, 2002). At this studio, Walt produced *Tommy Tucker's Tooth*, commissioned by a local dentist (Burnes, Butler & Viets, 2002).

In January 1923, when Walt could not afford rent, he began sleeping at the studio. Laugh-O-gram went bankrupt in 1923 after Walt's departure for California (personal communication, D. Smith, July 5, 2017).

"It is good to have a failure while you're young because it teaches you so much. For one thing it makes you aware that such a thing can happen to anybody, and once you've lived through the worst, you're never quite as vulnerable afterward," stated Walt Disney (Smith, 1994, p. 55).

In November 1995, Walt's daughter, Diane Disney Miller (with her husband Ron), toured the McConahy Building (Burnes, Butler & Viets, 2002).

In 1995, Thank You Walt Disney was formed. Thank You Walt Disney, Inc. has purchased the property with plans to transform the building. In 2014, the cost estimate for restoration was $2 million to $5 million (Alonzo, 2014).

On May 2, 2009, the existing murals were painted on the exterior (Thankyouwaltdisney.org, n.d.). The building is listed on the National Register of Historic Places (Burnes, Butler & Viets, 2002).

Walt Disney's grandson, Walter Elias Disney Miller, said, "This [the McConahy Building] is a part of history that can't be replaced. This building was the start of an amazing career and legacy. Walt was in Kansas City when everyone else in animation was in New York; what he started in that little building became the greatest animation studio ever" (Burnes, Butler, & Viets, 2002, p. 185).

For more information about this project, visit thankyouwaltdisney.org

Mrs. Boland's Boarding House

3241 Troost Avenue
Kansas City MO 64109

Significance: Temporary housing location for Walt.

Walt lived here temporarily after the house on Bellefontaine was sold (Burnes, Butler & Viets, 2002). Walt's brother, Herbert and Walt's parents moved to Portland, Oregon in November 1921 (Burnes, Butler & Viets, 2002).

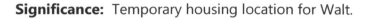

Muehlbach Hotel

(Now the Kansas City Marriott Downtown)
200 West 12th Street
Kansas City MO 64105
(816) 421-6800
marriott.com/hotels/travel/mcidt-kansas-city-marriott-downtown/

Significance: Walt and Lillian stayed here in 1931 on one of their vacations while they were en route to Washington, D.C. (see Chapter 64) (Thomas, 1998). According to a letter from Roy O. Disney to his parents: "...in Kansas City they would not let him spend a cent, and put him up at the Muehlbach Hotel, in a suite of rooms that had three baths. Walt and Lilly were kept busy all the time trying to keep three bathrooms busy" (Thomas, 1998, p. 91).

National Restaurant Association

(Now home to Midwest Litigation Services)
Mutual Building
1301 Oak Street
Kansas City MO 64106

Significance: One of Walt's work locations.

According to Susanin (2011), Walt established a small studio in an unused bathroom in the National Restaurant Association headquarters. This was for Iwerks-Disney to create the artwork for the *Restaurant News* (Susanin, 2011).

Newman Theatre

1116 Main Street
Kansas City MO 64105

Significance: Walt's very first client of his films in Kansas City.

Walt's first Laugh-O-gram debuted at Newman on March 20, 1921 (Burnes, Butler & Viets, 2002). Unfortunately, Walt sold his movies at cost, not making a profit (Burnes, Butler & Viets, 2002). "The Newman was one of Kansas City's more prominent theaters" (Burnes, Butler & Viets, 2002, p. 91).

"Typical local problems, such as Kansas City's road conditions and corruption in the police force, were the subjects of the approximately one-minute shorts" (Smith, 2006, p. 490).

Railway Exchange Building

705 Walnut Street
Kansas City MO 64106

Significance: One of the locations of Iwerks-Disney.

According to Susanin (2011), Iwerks-Disney moved out of the National Restaurant Association "bathroom" and into space at the Railway Exchange Building. "Their names were even listed on the building directory in the lobby" (Miller, 1956, p. 57).

Swope Park

3999 Swope Parkway & East Meyer Boulevard
Kansas City MO 64132
(816) 513-7500
kcparks.org/park/swope-park

Significance: A hang-out place for Walt.

Walt and his friends would relax in a wooden cabin (Burnes, Butler & Viets, 2002). On April 2, 1922, Walt was photographed there with his friend, Marion Cauger. "Walt and his friends often clowned around for gag shots" (Walt Disney Family Museum photo caption).

Temporary Apartment in a House #1

3415 Charlotte Street
Kansas City MO 64109

Significance: Temporary housing location for Walt.

Walt lived here temporarily after the house on Bellefontaine was sold (Burnes, Butler & Viets, 2002).

Temporary Apartment in a House #2

1325 Linwood Avenue
Kansas City MO 64109

Significance: Temporary housing location for Walt.

Walt lived here temporarily after the house on Bellefontaine was sold (Burnes, Butler & Viets, 2002).

Union Station

30 West Pershing Road
Kansas City MO 64108
(816) 460-2000
unionstation.org

Admission to the station building is free, but there is a charge for the attractions.

Significance: Walt arrived/departed on trains from/to here and he used to shower here. He left Kansas City for good in 1923, bound for California.

Walt Disney was a frequent visitor at Union Station. In 1911, Walt and his family arrived on a train from Marceline to Kansas City at the old Union Depot in the West Bottoms of Kansas City (Burnes, Butler & Viets, 2002). In the summer of 1917, Walt worked as a news butcher for the Van Noy Interstate News Co. He would pick up his supplies at the Van Noy office in Union Station and "then set up shop at the front of the train's smoking car" (Burnes, Butler & Viets, 2002, p. 57). Walt sold items on the Missouri-Pacific Railroad route from Kansas City to Jefferson City, MO (Burnes, Butler & Viets, 2002). In 1919, upon returning to Kansas City, he arrived on train and was met by Roy (Burnes, Butler & Viets, 2002).

When Walt was living in the Laugh-O-gram Films studio, he would shower at Union Station (Thomas, 1994).

"Once a week he would pay a dime to take a bath at Union Station" (Green, 2014, p. 19). In the summer of 1923, Walt boarded a California Limited train to Hollywood from Union Station. He bought a first class ticket, had $40 in his pocket, along with his suitcase, a few clothes and some drawing materials as he had sold his camera (Burnes, Butler & Viets, 2002).

In October 1931, Walt returned to Union Station, arriving by train, to accept a Legion of Honor award from DeMolay (Burnes, Butler & Viets, 2002). For more information about DeMolay, see pages 230-231). In early May 1936, Walt spent 20 minutes at Union Station (Burnes, Butler & Viets, 2002).

In June 1935, Walt, Lillian, Roy, and Edna passed through Kansas City on a train from Los Angeles to New York, en route to their vacation in Europe (Madden, 2017).

Tribute to Walt

On the second floor of Union Station is an exhibit that includes a tribute to Walt Disney. The title of the tribute is "Walt Disney's Other Dream."

 Download the Living History app in itunes for a Walt Disney interactive experience with your smartphone.

For more information:
itunes.apple.com/us/app/living-history-union-station-kansas-city/id930737689?mt=8

Meal Recommendation: Harvey's

 While you are at Union Station, have breakfast, brunch or lunch at Harvey's, located inside Union Station. harveyskc.com

Suggestion: If possible, leave Union Station as your last stop in Kansas City, similar to Walt's final stop in 1923.

University of Missouri-Kansas City

Student Union
5100 Cherry Street
Kansas City MO 64110
(816) 235-1000
umkc.edu

Significance: Walt designed the school's original mascot logo.

Photo by Jacob
Smallegan

In the Student Union is a window of a kangaroo drawing by Walt Disney (personal communication, Jacob Smallegan, 2017). In 1937, Walt Disney was asked "to draw an appropriate kangaroo for the University of Missouri-Kansas," which he did (Burnes, Butler & Viets, 2002). Walt Disney provided a kangaroo drawing shaking hands with Mickey Mouse, along with Walt's autograph (Burnes, Butler & Viets, 2002). Kasey the Kangaroo first appeared in the school newspaper of the University of Kansas City (as it was known then) in 1936 (Moreno, 2012).

"The story of his connection to the university starts in the fall of 1936. Our debate team was getting ready to compete against another university and some student suggested that we needed a mascot. The KC Zoo had just built a kangaroo exhibit and the progress of the exhibit had been in the paper all summer. Someone suggested that the Kangaroo would be a good mascot since KCU rhymed with Kangaroo. Half of the students liked the idea and half didn't think it was dignified enough. Some of the students who liked the idea formed a student political party called the Kangaroo party and part of their platform was to adopt the Kangaroo as our mascot. In support of their party's efforts several students who had earlier started the University News started a campus humor magazine called *The Kangaroo*. The Kangaroo party won the election and ever since the

Kangaroo has been our mascot. Sometime in 1937 one of these students wrote to Walt Disney and asked if he would draw a cover. My guess is that this person was student Howard Luck Gossage, who was the founding editor of the magazine and would later on move to San Francisco to start an advertising agency. His agency did business with Disney later. Disney did draw a cover for the magazine which was on the Spring '38 issue. The Casey Roo that has been used by the university ever since as the "Disney Roo" was actually the work of a student in the late 1930s based on the Disney drawing" (personal communication with Chris Wolff, January 23, 2017).

Wirthman Building

Corner of 31st and Troost Avenue
Kansas City MO 64109

Significance: Where Walt did some of his early film work. This building housed the Isis Theatre and it is where Laugh-O-gram Films moved into when it left the McConahy Building (Burnes, Butler & Viets, 2002).

Check out these books about Walt's life in Kansas City:

Walt Before Mickey
By Timothy Susanin

Walt Disney's Missouri: The Roots of a Creative Genius
(out of print)
By Brian Burnes, Dan Viets, and Robert W. Butler

The Adventures of Young Walt Disney
By William Silvester, Published by Theme Park Press

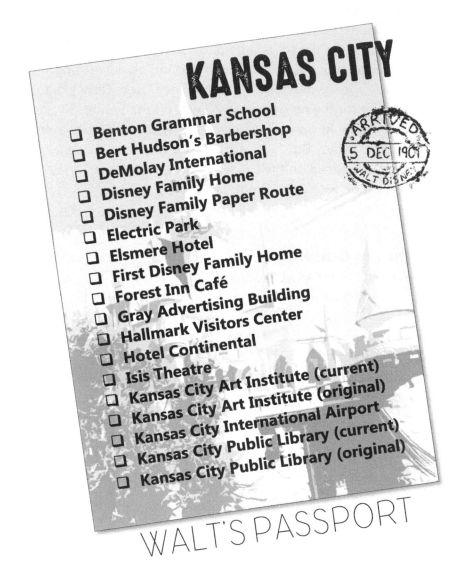

KANSAS CITY

- ❏ Benton Grammar School
- ❏ Bert Hudson's Barbershop
- ❏ DeMolay International
- ❏ Disney Family Home
- ❏ Disney Family Paper Route
- ❏ Electric Park
- ❏ Elsmere Hotel
- ❏ First Disney Family Home
- ❏ Forest Inn Café
- ❏ Gray Advertising Building
- ❏ Hallmark Visitors Center
- ❏ Hotel Continental
- ❏ Isis Theatre
- ❏ Kansas City Art Institute (current)
- ❏ Kansas City Art Institute (original)
- ❏ Kansas City International Airport
- ❏ Kansas City Public Library (current)
- ❏ Kansas City Public Library (original)

ARRIVED 15 DEC 1901 WALT DISNEY

WALT'S PASSPORT

KANSAS CITY

- ☐ Kansas City Slide Co./Film Ad. Co.
- ☐ Kaycee Studios (1)
- ☐ Kaycee Studios (2)
- ☐ Laugh-O-gram Films
- ☐ Mrs. Boland's Boarding House
- ☐ Muehlbach Hotel
- ☐ National Restaurant Association: Mutual Building
- ☐ Newman Theatre
- ☐ Railway Exchange Building
- ☐ Swope Park
- ☐ Temporary Apartment (House 1)
- ☐ Temporary Apartment (House 2)
- ☐ Union Station
- ☐ University of Missouri-Kansas City
- ☐ Wirthman Building

WALT'S PASSPORT

253

254

Chapter 53
Marceline, Missouri
The Hometown of Walt Disney

15 sites to explore

Walt Lived Here: 1906-1910
Walt's Later Visits: 1946, 1956, and 1960

"To tell the truth, more things of importance happened to me in Marceline than have happened since – or are likely to in the future"
–Walt Disney (Eisterhold Associates, Inc., 2001, n.p.).

Disney Farm
200 West Broadway Street
Marceline MO 64658

This site is open daily from sunrise to sunset. Closed for special events.

Significance: The farm where Walt Disney would play and draw during his time in Marceline. He would often draw under The Dreaming Tree (see next page).

The farm has Walt's Barn, Son of Dreaming Tree, and the Disney Arboretum.

Disney-themed signs lead you from the road to Walt's Barn, passing by Son of Dreaming Tree.

Walt's Barn

"The barn in Marceline was the setting for Walt's first venture as a showman. He dressed some of his pets and farm animals in costumes and announced the 'Disney Circus' to neighborhood kids charging 10 cents for admission. His audience left unimpressed and Walt's mother made him refund the admission fees. Walt learned a valuable lesson: 'Give the audience more than they expect and they'll be happy customers.' Walt's barn came home again in 2001 during a 3-day-old-fashioned barn raising. Guests from all over the world have left their message to Walt on the interior walls of the barn. Open daily sunrise to sunset. Closed for special events" (WDHM, 2017b, n.p.).

Visitors can sign inside Walt's Barn.
Bring a Black Sharpie Marker with you.

Dreaming Tree/ Son of Dreaming Tree

"Although Walt's original Dreaming Tree fell in 2015, you can still sense the energy that emanates from its location. Under its once majestic braces, Walt and Ruth Disney would observe the local nature that surrounded them. It was a magical location where Walt first learned to draw, write and dream. In 2004, Walt's grandson

[Brad Lund] planted a sapling no more than 30 feet from the original cottonwood. 'Son of Dreaming Tree' came from a seed harvested from the original tree, and that direct ancestor still grows proudly on the Disney Farm" (WDHM, 2017b, n.p.).

Disney Farm Arboretum

"In 2002, a Disney Farm tradition began when Toonfest Headliners planted the arboretum's first trees. Donated by American Forest Historic Tree Nursery, the trees come from historic properties all over the world and have a tie to Disney. For example, Walt was an admirer of Abraham Lincoln and there are trees from Lincoln's property" (WDHM, 2017b, n.p.).

Walt once considered a project in Marceline: a "turn-of-the-century working farm that doubled as a tourist attraction" to pay tribute to his hometown (Emerson, 2010, p. 12). However, that project fizzled after Walt's death, primarily due to other competing projects like CalArts and Walt Disney World.

E.P. Ripley Park

200 North Main Street
Marceline MO 64658

Significance: A 4-acre park that Walt Disney played in as a child.

"Ruth Disney often wrote of the band concerts the family attended in this park" (Eisterhold Associates, 2001, p. 32). "Walt named one of the first steam locomotives at Disneyland 'The E.P. Ripley'" (Eisterhold Associates, 2001, p. 32).

In 1898, the Santa Fe donated land in the center of the town for a park.

The park houses a steam engine that Walt visited in 1956.

Last Marceline Residence of the Disney Family
508 North Kansas Avenue
Marceline MO 64658

Significance: Walt's family rented a house here before moving to Kansas City, Missouri (Silvester, 2014).

Main Street, U.S.A.
(Kansas Avenue)
Downtown Marceline

Significance: Part of the inspiration of Main Street, U.S.A. in Disneyland and the other theme parks with a Fantasyland came from downtown Marceline (along with downtown Ft. Collins, Colorado).

Marceline has installed "Main Street, U.S.A." street signs downtown on Kansas Avenue.

The Allen Hotel on Main Street inspired Hotel Marceline in Disneyland (Plaque on Allen Hotel in Marceline). See page 29 about Hotel Marceline.

Park School

Corner of Chestnut and Ritchie
Marceline MO 64658

Significance: Walt attended elementary school here starting at age 7.

"Elias Disney decreed that it was more convenient for the boy [Walt] to wait until Ruth (Walt's sister) was old enough for school, and Walt was almost seven before he was enrolled at the Park School, a two-story red-brick building with two hundred students in grade and high school. Walt read the standard text, the McGuffey Eclectic Reader, and studied arithmetic, writing, geography and spelling. His grades were only fair, because he was always finding things that interested him more than schoolwork" (Thomas, 1994, p. 29).

Walt's first teacher was Miss Brown (Eisterhold Associates, 2001).

Walt Disney Elementary School

420 East California Avenue
Marceline MO 64658
(660) 376-2166
disney.marcelineschools.org

Significance: Walt dedicated this new elementary school and contributed some Disney themed items for the school.

"School officials in Marceline asked Walt Disney if he would allow them to use his name for the new school. Even though this was not the first public school named after him, Walt was thrilled. He not only said yes, but also contributed educational materials, artwork, playground equipment, and even a special flagpole to the new school" (Weiss, 2014, n.p.).

FLAGPOLE DONATED BY
WALT DISNEY
Walt Disney served as the Chairman of Pageantry for the 1960 Olympic Winter Games in Squaw Valley. According to Weiss (2014): "At the Olympic site, 30 flagpoles flew the flags of the 30 participating nations. Each flagpole had a plaque signed by Walt Disney" (n.p.). Walt donated one of those flagpoles, which is in front of the school. See page 97 for more information on Squaw Valley.

What's Inside
(not available for viewing by the public):

DISNEY CHARACTER ARTWORK
"Walt Disney commissioned one of his artists, Bob Moore, to design artwork for the school's entrance, hallway, and gymnasium. The artwork, featuring dozens of Disney characters, is delightful. The characters are rendered in a clean, simple style that reflects the Disney art of the era" (Weiss, 2014, n.p.).

PHOTOS OF WALT
Throughout the lobby, there are framed photos of Walt Disney during his visit to Walt Disney Elementary School.

MICKEY MOUSE TRIBUTE
On the floor in the lobby of the school is a tribute to Mickey Mouse, which was a gift of Inez and Rush Johnson, who hosted Walt Disney on one of his visits to Marceline.

HONORARY HIGH SCHOOL DIPLOMA
In the lobby of the school is a plaque that reads:
"On October 16, 1960, Walt was issued an honorary high school diploma from Marceline R-V High School. Walt never graduated from high school as he enlisted for service in the Red Cross during WWI and upon return entered the work force"
(Photo of plaque).

For a list of all Walt Disney Elementary Schools, see pages 341-342.

Walt Disney Hometown Museum

(in the former Santa Fe Railroad Depot)
120 East Santa Fe Avenue
Marceline MO 64658
(660) 376-3343
info@waltdisneymuseum.org
waltdisneymuseum.org

The Walt Disney Hometown Museum is open from April 1 to October 31 each year and is closed on Mondays.

Significance: This museum presents information about Walt's time in Marceline, Missouri, along with information about his family.

The Walt Disney Hometown Museum is located in the restored Santa Fe Railroad Depot. It opened in 2001. Many of the artifacts were donated by the family of Ruth Flora Disney Beecher, Walt's sister. The museum was started by Kaye Malins, whose family hosted Walt and Lillian Disney on their return visit to Marceline.

The Museum contains Walt's desk from Park School in Marceline, where he carved his initials.

Mission:
"Ensuring that the world never forgets that Walt Disney was a simple farm boy from Marceline who grew up to become the keeper of childhood magic" (WDHM, 2017c, n.p.).

"The Walt Disney Hometown Museum contains a unique collection of Disney family effects, not able to be viewed anywhere else in the world. Visitors to the museum are treated to interpretive exhibits focusing on the Disney family, Walt's life in Marceline as well as friends and family who supported him in his creative adventures while growing up. Also exhibited at the museum are hundreds of personal letters written between Disney family members, the only park attraction to leave and be operated outside of a Disney park and other artifacts, effects and personal belongings from Disney family members" (WDHM, 2017c, n.p.).

Walt Disney "A Day to Dream"

According to State of Missouri statute (House Bill 874): "October sixteenth of each year shall be known and designated as Walt Disney – 'A Day to Dream' Day. The citizens of this state are encouraged to participate in appropriate activities and events to commemorate the life and accomplishments of Walt Disney" (Missouri Revised Statutes, August 28, 2016, n.p.).

The Walt Disney Hometown Museum celebrates the State of Missouri's "Walt Disney 'Day to Dream' Day" in which kids and schools are invited to use a participation kit for suggested activities. This "Day to Dream" started in 2015.

Walt Disney Municipal Park and Swimming Pool

700 North Kansas Avenue
Marceline MO 64658
(660) 376-3528
marcelinemo.us/residents/parks_recreation.html

Significance: This park and pool are named in honor of Walt Disney.

The park was dedicated on July 4, 1956. Walt, Lillian, Roy and Edna Disney all attended. The swimming pool was also named for Walt. That swimming pool was replaced in 2016-2017 (Eisterhold Associates, 2001).

That park was also the site of Autopia.

"The park was once home to Midget Autopia, a retired Disneyland ride personally gifted by Walt and Roy in 1966...

The ride successfully ran in Marceline until 1977 when it was eventually retired from use. The track was removed in the summer of 2016" (WDHM, 2017c, n.p.).

Walt Disney Post Office Building

120 East Ritchie Avenue
Marceline MO 64658-9998
(800) 275-8777

To locate hours, visit tools.usps.com

Significance: A federal building named after Walt Disney, honoring his legacy and time in Marceline.

Special Walt Disney postmark available:
Where the Dream Began.

On September 11, 1968, the United States Postal Service issued a 6 cent stamp honoring Walt Disney. Walt Disney Productions staff members C. Robert Moore and Paul E. Wenzel were responsible for the design and portrait on the stamp (Bergen, May 8, 2015).

On the outside of the building is a plaque commemorating that occasion.

Stamp Day Parade

On September 11, 1968, Roy, Edna, Lillian and other family members traveled to Marceline for the issuing of the Walt Disney stamp and they participated in the parade.

On November 11, 2003, by Public Law 108-110, the U.S. Congress renamed the Marceline Main Post Office as the Walt Disney Post Office Building (U.S. Congress, November 11, 2003). Inside the post office is a plaque noting the 2003 naming.

TIP: Purchase postcard or Forever stamps in advance to save time. Have your postcards written out in advance.

Walt's Boyhood Home
100 West Broadway Street
Marceline MO 64658-1029

Significance: Walt lived here with his family from 1906 until 1910.

This is a private residence. Please respect the homeowners.

The home has an addition on it since Walt lived here. The home is now owned by Kaye Malins, who helped start the Walt Disney Hometown Museum.

When Walt lived here, there was no electricity or running water (Thomas, 1998).

About Kaye Malins
"Walt Disney stayed at Kaye's home (not this home) in 1956 for the dedication of the Walt Disney Swimming Pool and Park, so Disney has always been a part of her life. She is a founding board member of the Walt Disney Hometown Museum and has served as Director since the opening in 2001" (WDHM, 2017a, n.p.).

Yellow Creek

Just west of 29859 Julep Road
Brookfield MO 64628
(Still a part of the greater Marceline MO area)

Significance: Walt, his friends, and his siblings hung out here as children.

"Yellow Creek was young Walt's favorite fishing spot. On hot summer days, Walt and Roy walked the few miles to Yellow Creek and cooled themselves in the slow-moving water. 'Sometimes, if Mrs. Disney would let him, we'd go fishing in the creek,' recalled Walt's boyhood friend, Clem Flickinger, who lived in the farmhouse across the road from Disney's farm. 'We'd catch catfish and bowheads. There was a place where the water was 4 or 5 feet deep, and me and Walt would take off our clothes and swim. In the winter, a whole bunch of us would go sledding and skating with a big bonfire to keep warm, said Clem. On his 1956 return to Marceline, Walt and Roy reminisced about past picnics, swimming, and fishing using sticks for fishing poles and safety pins for hooks. Walt was filmed flicking a little fish a young boy who was standing on the bridge had just pulled from the creek" (Sampson, March 18, 2009, n.p.).

Farm/House of Erastus Taylor

31866 Julep Road
Marceline MO 64658

This is a private residence; please be respectful.

Significance: The Taylors were neighbors to the Disneys. Erastus Taylor was a Civil War veteran and known as "Grandpa Taylor." He and his wife, Elizabeth, lived here (Silvester, 2014).

"Walt visited the nearby farm of Erastus Taylor and listened to the Civil War veteran recount the battles of Shiloh and Bull Run" (Thomas, 1998, p. 29). On Sundays, Walt and his family would ride a buggy down to the house of the Taylors. Elias would play his fiddle. "Walt sat on a straight-backed chair throughout the concert, enthralled by the music and astonished by this unexpected aspect of his father" (Thomas, 1998, p. 29).

The Johnson Family Home

905 North Kansas Street
Marceline MO 64658

Significance: This was where Walt and Lillian Disney (along with Roy O. and Edna Disney) stayed during Walt's 1956 return visit to Marceline (see page 266 for information on that 1956 visit). It was the home of Rush and Inez Johnson, parents of Kaye Malins (see page 264). They hosted the Disneys because they were the only home in Marceline with air conditioning at the time. Walt slept in Kaye's bedroom.

Walt's Later Visits to Marceline

(WDHM, n.d.)

1946 – Walt returns to Marceline to refresh his memory for a project he is planning.

1956 – Walt and Roy Disney return to Marceline to dedicate the Walt Disney Swimming Pool and Park. They also visited Yellow Creek (see page 266).

 Walt and Roy hold the Midwest premiere of *The Great Locomotive Chase* at the Uptown Theatre. During remarks Walt tells the children of Marceline, "You are lucky to live in Marceline, my best memories are the years I spent here." Walt conceived the idea of purchasing his boyhood home and farm to develop a rural experience around it. RETLAW (Walter backwards) begins purchasing land for the Marceline Project.

1960 – Walt returns to Marceline to dedicate the Walt Disney Elementary School. At the dedication Walt states, "I'm not a funny guy, I'm just a farm boy from Marceline who hides behind a duck and a mouse." Walt donates a flag pole from the Squaw Valley Olympics, and a Disney artist decorates the interior of the school with Disney murals.

1967: December 15, 1967 (one year anniversary of Walt's death) was declared Walt Disney Memorial Day in Marceline by the town's mayor, Robert W. Smith. That commemoration even included a "Walt Disney Memorial Prayer" written by Rev. Fred J. Barnett, Pastor (Photo of Proclamation, Walt Disney Hometown Museum).

To learn more about Walt's time in Marceline, check out *The Adventures of Young Walt Disney* by William Silvester, published by Theme Park Press.

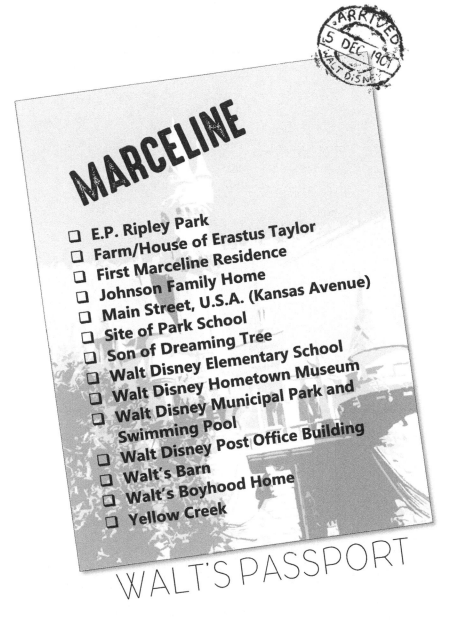

ARRIVED
5 DEC 1901
WALT DISNEY

MARCELINE

- ☐ E.P. Ripley Park
- ☐ Farm/House of Erastus Taylor
- ☐ First Marceline Residence
- ☐ Johnson Family Home
- ☐ Main Street, U.S.A. (Kansas Avenue)
- ☐ Site of Park School
- ☐ Son of Dreaming Tree
- ☐ Walt Disney Elementary School
- ☐ Walt Disney Hometown Museum
- ☐ Walt Disney Municipal Park and Swimming Pool
- ☐ Walt Disney Post Office Building
- ☐ Walt's Barn
- ☐ Walt's Boyhood Home
- ☐ Yellow Creek

WALT'S PASSPORT

Chapter 54
St. Louis, Missouri

Walt visited St. Louis several times:
1930, 1963, and 1964

1930:
"Walt consulted a doctor, who advised him to leave the studio and seek a complete rest. Walt and Lilly decided to take their first non-business trip since their honeymoon, five years before. Roy took charge of the studio, and Walt and Lilly left to fulfill his ambition on his return from France: to voyage down the Mississippi River. But when they visited the St. Louis waterfront, they discovered that only barges floated down the Mississippi" (Thomas, 1994, p. 104).

 They departed from St. Louis on a train for their first trip to Washington, D.C. (Thomas, 1994). For more information on their visit to Washington, D.C., see Chapter 64.

In 1963, St. Louis leaders asked Walt to create a film about St. Louis' history to honor the 200th anniversary of its founding in 1764. But Walt was interested in an attraction instead (Burnes, Butler & Viets, 2002).

Riverfront Square
The Non-Existing "Midwestern Disneyland"
(The St. Louis Project)
Proposed between Broadway and 7th Street
disneyhistoryinstitute.com/2013/03/walt-disne-and-riverfront-square-part-3.html

Significance: On May 19, 1963, Walt, Lillian, Sharon (daughter), and Sharon's then-husband, Robert Brown, arrived in St. Louis on a private plane for a May 20 tour of St. Louis (Burnes, Butler & Viets, 2002).

May 20, 1963
"The idea is clearly not with Walt as he met the Mayor of St. Louis in March, nor when he directed his economics firm— ERA—to create a feasibility study on Riverfront Square as a community mall that would also include one film-based Disney attraction. But the idea seems to be percolating—if only in small ways—by late spring, 1963" (Pierce, March 25, 2013, n.p.).

"For two hours they toured the Riverfront District, venturing down to the water where the twin arms of the Arch lifted toward a paper-white sky, the two metal limbs not yet connected. Members of the CCRC took Walt to the top of neighboring buildings, so Walt could visualize the placement of the Square in relationship to the rest of the city. They toured areas around the stadium, including the block identified as Riverfront Square" (Pierce, March 25, 2013, n.p.).

In August 1963, Buzz Price publicly shared the feasibility report, which indicated that Riverfront Square "could be self-supporting and potentially could show a modest profit" (Burnes, Butler & Viets, 2002, p. 144).

On November 18, 1963, Walt returned to St. Louis to clarify he was interested, but not committed to the project quite yet and held a press conference (Burnes, Butler & Viets, 2002).

"Originally slotted as a full city block (300 feet in length), plans now called for a super-block (600-feet in length). Originally filled with single-story, freestanding shops and restaurants, Riverfront Square would now likely be a massive enclosed structure—two city blocks, all indoors" (Pierce, March 25, 2013, n.p.).

"Early in 1965, plans were still on-track to build Riverfront Square, with Walt Disney creating good will in St. Louis by loaning out thirty-three Disneyland costumes (of Mickey, Minnie, the Seven Dwarfs, etc.) for a ten-day charity event. That year, the annual St. Louis Police Department's circus featured dozens of Disney characters, interspersed between traditional tightrope and trapeze acts, with all money raised going to the Police Officers' Relief Association. Likewise, Walt approved plans to feature Disney characters in the annual Veiled Prophet Parade— which was more-or-less the St. Louis version of a Mardi Gras festival" (Pierce, April 29, 2013, n.p.).

"The plan called for a town square patterned after Disneyland's Main Street, a combination of old St. Louis and New Orleans, with exhibits depicting the history of St. Louis as the Gateway to the West. But the project would have called for the investment of between $30 million and $50 million, and the deal fell through" (Saint Louis Post-Dispatch, November 17, 1978, p. 56).

Walt Disney issued a personal statement:
"We were asked to try to develop a major attraction having the impact on the St. Louis area of a Disneyland. We suggested at the outset that a project of that scope, in size and cost, might well prove difficult to accomplish, due to a number of imponderable factors. Such has proved to be the case" (Pierce, April 29, 2013, n.p.).

Municipal Opera

(The St. Louis Municipal Opera)
aka "The Muny"
Located in Forest Park
1 Theatre Drive
St. Louis MO 63112
(314) 361-1900
muny.org

Significance: Walt and Lillian visited this performance space on May 20, 1963.

"At the end of the tour [of St. Louis], Walt visited the city's Municipal Opera, where he noticed the stage included a circular rotating platform, which allowed the opera to keep multiple sets on the stage and turn them, one at a time, out to face the audience" (Pierce, March 25, 2013, n.p.).

During that visit, Walt suggested that The Muny produce *Snow White and the Seven Dwarfs* (Burnes, Butler & Viets, 2002).

Bel Air East Motel

(Now a Holiday Inn)
811 North 9th Street
St. Louis MO 63101

Significance: On March 16, 1964 at the Bel Air East Motel in St. Louis, Walt Disney and his designers held a series of meetings to both present the Disney vision for the St. Louis park and to discuss costs—specifically how costs would be divided up between the city, the CCRC and Disney (Pierce, April 22, 2013).

"There Disney gave the most detailed presentation yet about his ideas for the St. Louis park, describing a development that would be completely contained within a single, multi-level building covering two city blocks. Disney also revealed his intention to rename the project" (Burnes, Butler & Viets, 2002, p. 149).

ST. LOUIS

☐ **Proposed site of Riverfront Square**
☐ **Site of the Bel Air East Motel**
☐ **The Muny**

ARRIVED
5 DEC 1961
WALT DISNEY

WALT'S PASSPORT

NEW JERSEY

Hoboken

 Food Available

 Guided Tour Available

 Not Open to the Public

 Original Structure Gone

 Train Connection

Parking Fee

 Post Death Tribute

Hotel

Must See

 Multimedia

 Admission Fee

 Drive By Location

Chapter 55
Hoboken, New Jersey

No specific site to see.

 Significance: Walt arrived on a train from Sound Beach, Connecticut to Hoboken, New Jersey while serving in the American Ambulance Corps. On November 18, 1918, Walt took a rusting cattle ship, the Vaubin, from Hoboken to France. The ship arrived in LeHavre, France on December 4. (Thomas, 1994).

To learn more about Walt's time in the American Ambulance Corps., read *In the Service of the Red Cross* by David Lesjak. Available from Theme Park Press.

NEW YORK

New York City Ⓦ

Food Available	Guided Tour Available	Not Open to the Public	Original Structure Gone	Train Connection	Parking Fee
Post Death Tribute	Hotel	Must See	Multimedia	Admission Fee	Drive By Location

Chapter 56
New York, New York
Metropolitan Area

Walt was a frequent visitor to New York City. He was there in 1919, 1928-1929, 1931, 1935, 1940-1941, 1943-1944, 1946-1947, 1949, 1951-1966, visiting in 28 years of his life (personal communication, D. Smith, July 5, 2017).

In 1919, Walt landed in New York after returning from his service with the American Ambulance Corps. in France. "He was stimulated by the size and energy of Manhattan, and he wandered the streets with unabashed awe of the high buildings" (Thomas, 1994, p. 53).

To learn more about Walt's time in the American Ambulance Corps., read *In the Service of the Red Cross* by David Lesjak. Available from Theme Park Press.

Algonquin Hotel

59 West 44th Street
New York NY 10036
(212) 840-6800
algonquinhotel.com

Significance: Walt and Lilly stayed here during a January 1930 visit to meet with Pat Powers regarding Cinephone (Thomas, 1994).

Colony Theater
(now the Broadway Theater)

1681 Broadway at 53rd Street
New York NY 10036
(212) 944-3700
shubert.nyc/theatres/broadway

Significance: The theater where *Steamboat Willie* opened on
November 18, 1928, which became the date for Mickey Mouse's
birthday (Thomas, 1994).

"The Colony Theatre was designed by architect Eugene DeRosa
and built for B.S. Moss. Opening on December 25, 1924, the
1,761-seat Colony was initially used as a movie palace, showing
Universal Pictures productions and vaudeville. In 1930 Moss
changed the name to Broadway Theatre and began staging
plays. The Shubert Organization purchased the Broadway in
1939, and the next year saw the opening of Walt Disney's
Fantasia, and, in 1941, the world premiere of Disney's *Dumbo*"
(Colony Theater, n.d.).

"A plaque was installed in the lobby at the time of Mickey
Mouse's 50th anniversary in 1978" (Smith, 2006, p. 93).

Hotel Knickerbocker

6 Times Square
New York NY 10036
(212) 204-4980
theknickerbocker.com

Significance: Walt stayed here in September and October 1928 (Thomas, 1994).

Day after Labor Day, 1928
Walt traveled to New York City to find a partner to add sound to his films.

October 26, 1928
Walt shared a room at the Knickerbocker with Stalling (Barrier, 2007).

Strand Theatre on Broadway

1579 Broadway
New York NY 10036

Significance: *The Barn Dance* debuted here. Walt saw the film at the Strand Theatre (Thomas, 1994).

"The Strand Theatre was an early movie palace located at 1579 Broadway, at the northwest corner of 47th Street and Broadway in Times Square, New York City. Opened in 1914, the theater was later known as the Mark Strand Theatre, the Warner Theatre, and the Cinerama Theatre. It closed as the RKO Warner Twin Theatre, and was demolished in 1987" (Strand Theatre, n.d., n.p.).

R.K.O. Building

1270 Sixth Avenue
New York NY 10020

Significance: Walt established a branch office here.

"For several months in 1936, the [Walt Disney] studio managed a branch office in New York, where they 'auditioned' new talent, specifically, animators. Walt said in a memo: 'I need 300 artists...find them'" (Walt Disney Family Museum plaque).

Flushing Meadows-Corona Park

Grand Central Parkway, Whitestone Expressway
Between 111 Street and College Point Boulevard, Park Drive East
Queens NY 11375
(718) 760-6565
nycgovparks.org/parks/flushing-meadows-corona-park

Significance: Site of the 1964-1965 World's Fair, where Walt had designed and introduced several exhibits.

Dates of the World's Fair:
April 22 to October 18, 1964
April 21 to October 17, 1965

"The Fair featured 140 pavilions spread across the 646 acres that had also served as the site of the 1939 New York's World Fair. Most of the pavilions were sponsored by United States commercial companies, but 21 states and 36 foreign countries were also represented. The theme of the 1964 World's Fair was 'Peace Through Understanding' and was devoted to 'Man on a Shrinking Globe in an Expanding Universe.' Developing exhibits for the Fair provided unique opportunities for Walt Disney and his Imagineers. Walt was interested in testing Disney entertainment with East Coast audiences to inform his decision on whether or not to build another park there. Walt also saw the opportunity for research and development for new attractions that could ultimately end up in Disneyland, but would be paid for on the dime of other corporations for the Fair. The Disney attractions were some of the most popular exhibits at the fair; 135,000 visitors per day visited Disney's four exhibits during the first season alone" (Carnaham, June 26, 2012, n.p.).

In 1960, the Disney team reached out to major corporations to offer to create their exhibits for the fair. Ford Motor Company, General Electric, the State of Illinois, and Pepsi-Cola accepted (Thomas, 1998).

GENERAL ELECTRIC'S PROGRESSLAND
This exhibit promoted the role of electricity in American life. The Broadway production *Our Town* inspired this attraction. A unique circular theater had six stages and served 3,600 guests an hour. (This became Walt Disney's Carousel of Progress in Tomorrowland at the Magic Kingdom. See pages 155-156) (Carnaham, June 26, 2012).

PEPSI COLA'S IT'S A SMALL WORLD
This exhibit was completed in nine months and was a nine-minute boat ride costing 95 cents for adults and 60 cents for children. The Sherman Brothers wrote the now very popular theme song. This attraction now appears in every Disney theme park (Carnaham, June 26, 2012).

STATE OF ILLINOIS' GREAT MOMENTS WITH MR. LINCOLN
This exhibit featured an Audio-Animatronics Abraham Lincoln who gave performances five times an hour. He delivered speeches on freedom, civil rights, and liberty. This exhibit inspired the Audio-Animatronics featured in Pirates of the Caribbean (Carnaham, June 26, 2012).

This exhibit is now housed in Disneyland on Main Street, U.S.A. in the Great Moments with Mr. Lincoln exhibit.

FORD'S MAGIC SKYWAY
This exhibit featured more than 150 1964 Ford Convertibles and showcased the progress of humans. Four languages were available through the car radio. Walt Disney actually narrated this attraction (Carnaham, June 26, 2012).

All but the Ford exhibit were transported from New York to Disneyland (Thomas, 1998).

"After the close of the Fair in 1965, the site was transformed into the park we know today, a favorite destination for millions of visitors. A large and diverse population uses the park each day for soccer and barbecuing, world-renowned art and professional sports teams, championship tennis, a row on the lake or a bike ride" (New York City Parks, n.d., n.p.).

 Video Virtual Tour:
nycgovparks.org/highlights/fmcp-worlds-fairs/virtual-video-tour

NEW YORK

- ☐ **Algonquin Hotel**
- ☐ **Colony Theater**
- ☐ **Flushing-Meadows-Corona Park**
- ☐ **Hotel Knickerbocker**
- ☐ **Strand Theater on Broadway**
- ☐ **R.K.O. Building**

ARRIVED
5 DEC. 1901
WALT DISNEY

WALT'S PASSPORT

OHIO

Ⓦ Steuben

Food Available	Guided Tour Available	Not Open to the Public	Original Structure Gone	Train Connection	Parking Fee

Post Death Tribute	Hotel	Must See	Multimedia	Admission Fee	Drive By Location

Chapter 57
Steuben, Ohio

Birthplace of Flora Call Disney, Walt's mother
1860 Greenfield
Steuben OH 44890

(Note: Address cannot be located in Google Maps.)

Significance: This is the town where Walt Disney's mother, Flora Call, was born on April 22, 1868 to Charles Call and Henrietta Gross (Flora Call Disney, n.d.). Charles and Henrietta became Walt's in-laws.

Steuben Cemetery
Now called Greenfield Township Cemetery
Monroeville OH 44847

Off of Route 162, right next to Church of the Master

Significance: Flora's grandfather, Eber Call, is buried in Steuben's cemetery (personal communication, D. Smith, July 5, 2017). He is located in Section 1, Row 7, #9 (findagrave.com, October 4, 2011).

STEUBEN

☐ **Town of Steuben**

ARRIVED
5 DEC 1901
WALT DISNEY

WALT'S PASSPORT

OREGON

W Portland

Food Available

Guided
Tour Available

Not Open to
the Public

Original Structure
Gone

Train
Connection

Parking
Fee

Post Death
Tribute

Hotel

Must See

Multimedia

Admission
Fee

Drive By
Location

Chapter 58
Portland, Oregon

Residence of Miss Ruth Disney (Walt's sister)
1618 Southeast Morrison Street
Portland OR 97214

Significance: Walt's sister, Ruth, was living here in September 1938, based on a letter that Walt wrote to Ruth (Correspondence at the Walt Disney Family Museum).

"Ruth was a connoisseur of organ music, purchasing and outfitting an old theater organ at her home" (Smith, 2006, p. 172).

Another Residence of
Mrs. Ruth (Disney) Beecher (Walt's sister)
916 Southeast 38th Avenue
Portland OR 97214

Significance: Walt's sister, Ruth, lived here at one time (Correspondence at the Walt Disney Family Museum).

Another Residence of
Mrs. Ruth (Disney) Beecher (Walt's sister)
1523 Northeast Sixth Avenue
Portland OR 97214

Significance: Walt's sister, Ruth, lived here at one time
(Correspondence at the Walt Disney Family Museum).

Residence of Elias and Flora Disney
1630 Southeast Morrison Street
Portland OR 97214

Significance: Walt and Lillian visited Elias and Flora Disney
(Walt's parents) in Portland in the summer of 1925, after their
honeymoon at Mt. Rainier National Park and Seattle,
Washington (Gabler, 2006).

Elias and Flora moved here from Kansas City in the Fall of 1921
(Winton, 2015).

Lincoln Memorial Park:
Gravesite of Ruth Disney
11801 Southeast Mount Scott Boulevard
Portland OR 97266
(800) 343-4464
dignitymemorial.com/lincoln-memorial-park-funeral-home/en-us/index.page

Significance: The burial site of Walt's sister, Ruth Flora Disney
Beecher. Ruth's tombstone reads: "Wife, Mother, Grandmother,
Beloved Sister of Walt Disney." Ruth died in 1995.

Ruth's grave is located in the Lincoln Terrace section, which is just past the Maplewood Cremation area. Her grave is located in Lot 346, Space #2.

Ruth is buried next to her husband (Theodore Charles Beecher), son (Theodore (Ted) Warren Beecher) and her daughter-in-law (Carolyn Beecher).

Herbert Disney, one of Walt's brothers, also lived in Portland for awhile, before moving to Los Angeles in 1930, where he delivered mail.

PORTLAND

☐ Morrison Street
☐ 38th Avenue
☐ Sixth Avenue
☐ Home of Flora and Elias
☐ Lincoln Memorial Park

ARRIVED
5 DEC 1901
WALT DISNEY

WALT'S PASSPORT

PENNSYLVANIA

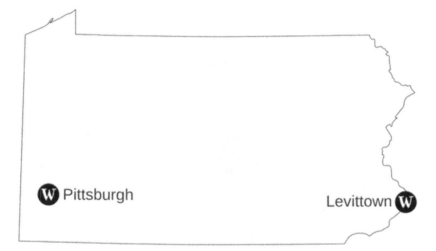

W Pittsburgh

Levittown W

 Food Available

 Guided Tour Available

 Not Open to the Public

 Original Structure Gone

 Train Connection

 Parking Fee

 Post Death Tribute

 Hotel

 Must See

 Multimedia

 Admission Fee

 Drive By Location

Chapter 59
Levittown, Pennsylvania

Walt Disney Elementary School

200 Lakeside Drive
Levittown PA 19054
(215) 949-6868
pennsbury.k12.pa.us/pennsbury/Pennsbury/www.pennsbury.k12.
pa.us/pennsbury/Disney/index.html

Significance: Walt attended the dedication of this school, named for him, on September 24, 1955. September 24 was declared "Walt Disney Day" in Pennsylvania by Governor George Leader (Lebo, 2010).

Photos Online:
statemuseumpa.org/levittown/two/j.html

This is one of the 15 Walt Disney Elementary Schools in the United States. For the complete list of all Walt Disney Elementary Schools, see pages 341-342.

LEVITTOWN

☐ **Walt Disney Elementary School**

ARRIVED
5 DEC. 1901
WALT DISNE

WALT'S PASSPORT

Chapter 60
Pittsburgh, Pennsylvania

Westinghouse Research Center

Now located at
1000 Westinghouse Drive
Suite 572A
Cranberry Township PA 16066

Significance: Walt flew to Pittsburgh on his company plane in 1966 and spent "three days at the Westinghouse Research Center, inspecting the company's rapid-transit system and other developments for the future" (Thomas, 1994, p. 344).

PITTSBURGH

☐ Westinghouse Research Center

WALT'S PASSPORT

VIRGINIA

Mount Vernon

Food Available

Guided
Tour Available

Not Open to
the Public

Original Structure
Gone

Train
Connection

Parking
Fee

Post Death
Tribute

Hotel

Must See

Multimedia

Admission
Fee

Drive By
Location

Chapter 61
Mt. Vernon, Virginia

Mt. Vernon

3200 Mount Vernon Highway
Mount Vernon VA 22121
mountvernon.org

Significance: Walt and Lillian visited there during their time in the Washington D.C. area during a 1930 vacation (see Chapter 64).

Mount Vernon was the plantation house of George Washington, the first President of the United States, and his wife, Martha Dandridge Custis Washington.

 mountvernon.org/site/virtual-tour

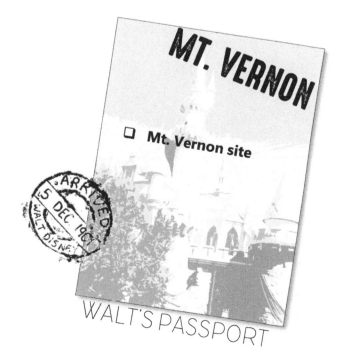

WASHINGTON

Seattle

Ashford

 Food Available

 Guided Tour Available

 Not Open to the Public

 Original Structure Gone

 Train Connection

 Parking Fee

 Post Death Tribute

 Hotel

 Must See

 Multimedia

 Admission Fee

 Drive By Location

Chapter 62
Ashford, Washington

Mt. Rainier National Park

39000 State Route 706 East
Ashford WA 98304
(360) 569-2211
nps.gov/mora/index.htm

Significance: Where Walt and Lillian honeymooned in July/August 1925. They also went to Seattle and Portland on their honeymoon.

ASHFORD

☐ **Mt. Rainier National Park**

WALT'S PASSPORT

ARRIVED
15 DEC 1961
WALT DISN

Chapter 63
Seattle, Washington

Significance: Where Walt and Lillian honeymooned in July/August 1925. Walt and his family visited the World's Fair in Seattle in September, 1962.

Seattle World's Fair/Century 21 Exposition
(now the Seattle Center area)

305 Harrison Street
Seattle WA 98109
(206) 684-7200
seattlecenter.com

According to Stein (2012), Walt and his family flew up from Los Angeles via United Airlines on September 21, 1962 to see the Seattle World's Fair. Walt was joined by Lillian, daughter Sharon Disney Brown, and her husband, Robert Brown. Walt visited this fair for fun, attending Friday, Saturday and Sunday (Stein, 2012).

Walt was given a Gold Pass for the Century 21 Exposition (personal communication, D. Smith, June 19, 2017). "Walt wrote to Joseph Grandy, President of the fair, "My Gold Pass did, indeed, stand us in very good stead as it was an open Sesame to everything we wanted to see" (personal communication, D. Smith, June 19, 2017).

"When he [Walt] visited on Saturday and Sunday, huge crowds followed him everywhere. When he wasn't signing autographs, he was often being interviewed by newspaper and television reporters" (Stein, 2012, n.p.).

"He seemed impressed with the Space Needle, predicting that there would be 'Space Needles cropping up all over after the success of this one'" (Stein, 2012, n.p.).

"The SPACE NEEDLE is terrific and it was thrilling to be sitting there eating Alaskan crab legs with the whole panorama of Seattle before you — a very beautiful sight," stated Walt (personal communication, D. Smith, June 19, 2017).

Seattle was where Walt saw a dentist and had a tooth pulled on his honeymoon (Miller, 1956).

WASHINGTON,
DISTRICT OF COLUMBIA

 Washington

Food Available

Guided
Tour Available

Not Open to
the Public

Original Structure
Gone

Train
Connection

Parking
Fee

Post Death
Tribute

Hotel

Must See

Multimedia

Admission
Fee

Drive By
Location

Chapter 64
Washington, D.C.

Mayflower Hotel (now a Marriott)

1127 Connecticut Avenue Northwest
Washington DC 20036
(202) 347-3000
marriott.com/hotels/travel/wasak-the-mayflower-hotel-autograph-collection/

 Significance: In 1930, Walt and Lilly took a train from St. Louis to Washington, D.C.; their first visit here. They stayed at the Mayflower Hotel. They were there for three days (Miller, 1956).

"Walt took Lilly to see the Washington Monument, Mount Vernon, the Lincoln Memorial and the Capitol" (Thomas, 1994, p. 104). (See Chapter 61 for information on Mt. Vernon.)

"Then they traveled by train down the Atlantic Coast to Key West and boarded a ship for Cuba" (Thomas, 1994, p. 104).

The White House
1600 Pennsylvania Avenue Northwest
Washington DC 20500
(202) 456-1111
whitehouse.gov

Significance: Walt was presented with the Medal of Freedom (the highest civilian honor) by President Lyndon B. Johnson at The White House on November 14, 1964 (Thomas, 1994). The citation states, "Artist and impresario, in the course of entertaining an age, Walt Disney has created an American folklore" (Thomas, 1994, p. 328).

Lincoln Memorial

2 Lincoln Memorial Circle Northwest
Washington DC 20037
(202) 426-6841
nps.gov/linc/index.htm

Walt and Lillian visited the Lincoln Memorial during a 1930 trip.

Significance: "Walt stood before the heroic statue of Lincoln for minutes, reading the measured words carved in marble as his eyes filled with tears" just before heading to The White House to receive his Medal of Freedom (Thomas, 1994, p. 327-328).

Washington Monument

Two 15th Street Northwest
Washington DC 20037
(202) 426-6841
nps.gov/wamo/index.htm

Significance: Walt and Lillian visited the Washington Monument during a 1930 trip.

United States Capitol

East Capitol Street Northeast & First Street Southeast
Washington DC 20004
(202) 226-8000
visitthecapitol.gov

Significance: Walt and Lillian visited the U.S. Capitol during a
1930 trip.

The Capitol Visitor Center, the main entrance to the U.S. Capitol,
is located beneath the East Front plaza of the U.S. Capitol at First
Street and East Capitol Street.

Cannon House Office Building

House Caucus Room
27 Independence Avenue Southeast
Washington DC 20003
aoc.gov/capitol-buildings/cannon-house-office-building

Significance: On October 24, 1947, Walt testified in front of the
House Committee on Un-American Activities (HUAC) "to decry
Communist influence in the labor unions that were responsible
for producing Hollywood's famous productions..."
(Frevele, 2015, n.p.).

General D.C. Area

In the 1940s, "Walt made frequent trips to Washington for dealings with the government. When he couldn't get a hotel reservation, he sat through several performances in a movie house in order to get some rest. During one of the Washington trips, he met with Frank Capra..." (Thomas, 1994, p. 179).

In December 1942, "John L. Sullivan, a Treasury Department official, telephoned Walt. Henry Morgenthau, the Secretary of the Treasury, had an urgent special project he wanted to discuss" (Thomas, 1994, p. 180). Walt made the flight. The Treasury Department had requested that Walt 'help sell people on paying income tax'" (Thomas, 1994, p. 180).

In late December 1942, Walt flew to Washington to show the storyboards to Morgenthau (Thomas, 1994).

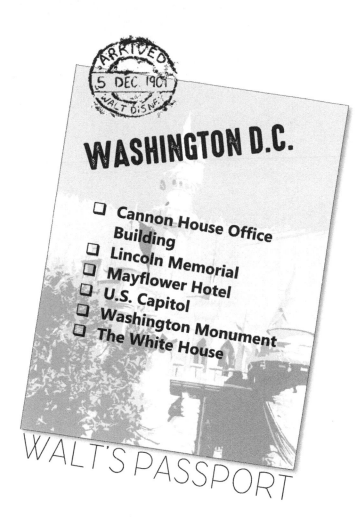

WASHINGTON D.C.

- ☐ Cannon House Office Building
- ☐ Lincoln Memorial
- ☐ Mayflower Hotel
- ☐ U.S. Capitol
- ☐ Washington Monument
- ☐ The White House

WALT'S PASSPORT

CANADA

ONTARIO

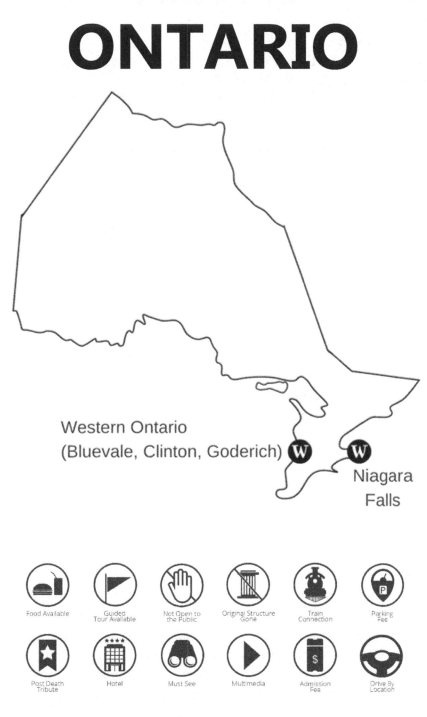

Western Ontario
(Bluevale, Clinton, Goderich) **W** **W**
Niagara
Falls

Food Available

Guided
Tour Available

Not Open to
the Public

Original Structure
Gone

Train
Connection

Parking
Fee

Post Death
Tribute

Hotel

Must See

Multimedia

Admission
Fee

Drive By
Location

Ontario, Canada

Significance:
In 1835, Arundel Disney (Walt's great-grandfather) arrived in Goderich Township (Korkis, 2017).
In 1859, Elias Disney (Walt's father) was born in Bluevale, Ontario.
In 1947, Walt and Lillian visited Canada to trace his family heritage (Korkis, 2017).

All of these sites in Western Ontario are in what is referred to as "Ontario's West Coast."

About Walt's Connections in Canada:
"Walt's family had strong family roots in Canada. Walt's great-grandfather Arundel Disney and his brother Robert sailed with their families in September 1834 from Liverpool, England, to begin a new life in America. Once they arrived, Robert went to the Midwest and began farming. Arundel traveled to the Canadian frontier in the Goderich Township, Ontario" (Korkis, 2017, n.p.).

Arundel built a mill beside the Maitland River and found success grinding wheat and sawing timber.

"Kepple Disney [Walt's grandfather] grew up helping in his father's mill near Holmesville and he married Mary Richardson in 1858. He was 25 and she was 18. Their marriage certificate shows that Kepple was already living in Morris, and that his parents were Elias and Maria [Swan] Disney. Mary was living in Goderich Township and her parents were Robert and Rose Richardson. Mary had family in this area. Her brother Joseph was establishing a homestead...[as was] her sister Elizabeth Cantelon. According to the 1861 census, Kepple and Mary were living here in a one-story log house with their two-year-old son, Elias. They were farmers, and at that time they had 15 acres of the farm under cultivation, and valued their land at $1,000, their farm implements at $12, and their livestock at $100. They planted their farm to wheat, oats and potatoes, and produced 300 pounds of maple sugar. The 1871 census shows that three of their children were in school, and that the family was Wesleyan Methodists. By this time, they had two barns, and their livestock included one milk cow, 10 sheep and two pigs. They also had a tenant, John Gillies. At times Kepple worked off the farm, drilling for oil in Lambton and he owned a salt well in Goderich for a while. Kepple and Mary had eleven children. The oldest children were born on this farm, and received their education at USS#4 Morris and Turnberry, and occasionally at Central Public School in Goderich, where they had extended family. Their children included Elias, Robert Samuel, Annie Maria (Irion), Edmond John, Albertha Mary (Johnson), Kepple, Elizabeth (Saunders), Adina (Jones) and William Harvey who were born before the family moved to the States, where two more children were born" (Municipality of Morris-Turnberry, 2012, page unknown).

In February 1859, Walt's father, Elias, was born to Arundel's eldest son Kepple on Jamestown Road near Bluevale, which was not too far from Goderich.

In 1856, the central school, now part of the Huron County Museum (see page 321), was erected. It was actually Elias Disney who attended school here, not Walt as often claimed. The building became a museum in 1951.

In 1877, Elias left Huron County with his father, who hated the Canadian winters, for the California gold rush, but they never made it there, as his father was convinced by a member of the Union Pacific Railroad to purchase a plot of land about 200 acres in Ellis, Kansas (see pages 199-200 for more information on Ellis). Elias, who was 18 years old at the time, and Robert (Walt's uncle who later helped Walt in California) accompanied their father, Kepple Disney.

Roy O. Disney, Edna Disney and Edna's niece, Lettye Vogel, made a "pilgrimage" to Elias Disney's birthplace in Canada in Fall 1948 (Thomas, 1998). They traveled 10,600 miles on that trip through 30 states (Thomas, 1998).

> *The Huron Expositor*
> *November 15, 1878*
>
> Bluevale – For Kansas – the family of Mr. Keppel Disney left here on Tuesday morning last [November 12, 1878] for Kansas. Mr. Disney was previously a farmer on concession 1, of Morris, he left here six months ago and purchased a large farm in the above state. A large number of their friends and neighbours accompanied them to the station, they being old residents, having lived here for the past 18 years. Mrs. Disney and family appeared deeply affected at parting with so many old acquaintances, but were nevertheless very anxious to be again with Mr. Disney. We wish them a very pleasant and successful trip.

Source:
A Harvest of Memories:
Volume I and II

Municipality of Morris-Turnberry (2012).

Chapter 65
Hamlet of Bluevale/Wingham
Ontario, Canada

Birthplace of Elias Disney

41338A Jamestown Road
Wingham ON Canada N0G 2W0

(This address may appear as the city of "Morris-Turnberry" in your GPS instead of Wingham.)

This part of Jamestown Road is a dirt road.

Significance: This is the birthplace of Walt Disney's father, Elias Disney.

Elias was born at 41338A Jamestown Road, close to the small Hamlet of Bluevale, Ontario, Canada. He was born to Irish Protestant immigrants Kepple Elias Disney (1832–1891) and Mary Richardson (1838–1909). Both parents had immigrated from Ireland to Canada as children, accompanying their parents.

There are no known monuments/markers connected to the Disney family in this area. Note that the house that stands there now is a private residence.

"In a 1963 interview with Fletcher Markle on the CBC Television program Telescope, Walt recounted a return visit to his father's hometown that he took with his wife, Lillian, after his father passed away:

'We got up there and she [Lillian Disney] really fell in love with the Town of Goderich. It was a beautiful town and she was quite happy about it. But I wanted to find my homestead where my grandfather went out and cut the trees down and pulled the rocks apart... where my father was born. So they gave me directions and everybody was trying to be helpful and everything and Mrs. Disney reluctantly went along and I found this old place and I said, 'This is it -- there.' It was really deserted. There were cows running through the house and chickens all around and I had my camera and I got out and photographed that thing from every angle. When I got through I found out I had photographed the wrong homestead. Ever since, Mrs. Disney has never forgot. She tells that story to everybody -- about when Walt went up to Canada and he photographed the wrong homestead!'" (Belobradic, April 22, 2017, n.p.).

Goderich Central School is where young Elias went to school (Belobradic, April 22, 2017). (See Chapter 66 for more information.)

If driving to Elias' birthplace from southwest Ontario, be sure to stop in the Historic Village of Blyth. The Queens Bakery is a must-visit, along with the new Cowbell Brewing Co. The Queens Bakery has three suites that can be rented for overnight accommodations.

queensbakery.ca
cowbellbrewing.com

Wingham, Ontario, Canada is the birthplace of Alice Munro, a Nobel Prize winning author.   For more information: biography.com/people/alice-munro-9418218

Bluevale Pioneer Cemetery

81 Bell Street
Bluevale ON Canada N0G 1G0

Significance: Walt references that he has relatives buried here: "'I've visited the Bluevale pioneer cemetery where my French-Irish grandparents were buried,' Disney says. 'I write often to my Canadian cousins living up there—the Richardsons and Pearsons. A Richardson keeps up the old log cabin where my grandmother and granddad were married. As for the Pearsons, I believe I'm related to Prime Minister Lester Pearson on my grandmother's side of the family'" (Jackson, November 30, 2005, p. 119).

However, a visit to this cemetery in 2017 with a look at every plot did not reveal any graves with "Richardson" or "Pearson" on them. Mary Richardson was Walt's paternal grandmother. Ruth and Robert Richardson were Walt's paternal great great grandparents.

Alexander Duncan deeded three acres of land for this cemetery around 1860. The Bluevale Cemetery Committee bought additional land for $25 to increase the cemetery to nearly four acres. In the early days, each family had the responsibility to dig the grave for the departed family member. By 1950, the cemetery condition had deteriorated so a "clean up bee" was held by the community to improve it.

There are no signs that identify this cemetery.

Wesley Methodist Church and Sunday School

Location Unknown

Significance: Where Elias Disney (Walt's father) attended Sunday church services (Korkis, 2017).

According to a 1939 interview with Elias:
"Our life and work were such as comes to boys and girls brought up on the farm – a pure and wholesome atmosphere, both physically and morally" (Korkis, 2017, n.p.).

Chapter 66
Goderich Township
Ontario, Canada
(Huron County)

Huron County Museum
110 North Street
Goderich ON Canada N7A 2T8
(519) 524-2686
huroncountymuseum.ca

Significance: This museum is in the old school building, where Elias Disney (Walt's father) attended school (Korkis, 2017).

Opened as a school in 1856. Became a museum in 1951 (Korkis, 2017).

Maitland Cemetery
35454 Huron Road
Goderich ON Canada
N7A 3X8
(519) 524-8344
townhall@goderich.ca

goderich.ca/en/townhall/cemetery.asp

Significance:
Robert and Jane Disney are buried here. Robert is Walt Disney's great grand uncle and Jane was his wife. Robert was the brother

of Arundel Elias Disney, who was Elias Disney's grandfather (Parker, 2017; Cruise, 2012).

The Maitland Cemetery is open approximately mid April to November, weather permitting. Office Hours are Monday to Friday 8 a.m. to 4 p.m.

Locating the Tombstone (Robert and Jane are together in one):

- Enter the cemetery and follow the winding road for .2 miles (passing the crypts on your left).
- Go to the left of the Map Station (grabbing a paper map is optional; however, the Disney grave is located in section E-7 of on the map).
- Head toward the white building with the green trim, going left of that building.
- Stop when you see the low grey tombstone with the name, "Watson" on it. Park there.
- Jane and Robert Disney's grave is about 11 spaces down from the Watson marker.

GODERICH

☐ **Huron County Museum**
☐ **Maitland Cemetery**

ARRIVED
5 DEC 1901
WALT DISNE

WALT'S PASSPORT

Chapter 67
Clinton
Ontario, Canada

Disney Road

37426-37750 Disney Road
Clinton ON Canada N0M 1L0

(Clinton may show up in the GPS as "Central Huron.")

This is a dirt road.
Enter from Maitland Line road, which is paved.

Significance: A road named after the Disney family.

CLINTON

☐ **Disney Road**

ARRIVED
5 DEC 1901
WALT DISNEY

WALT'S PASSPORT

Chapter 68
Niagara Falls
Ontario, Canada

Seagram Tower

(Now The Tower Hotel)
6732 Fallsview Boulevard
Niagara Falls ON Canada L2G 3W6
(866) 325-5784
niagaratower.com

Significance: "Another of these early projects was the Seagram Tower on the Canadian side of Niagara Falls. This project was discussed early in 1963, with Walt flying to Niagara that summer to meet with Franklin Miller, mayor of the city, and business leaders, to discuss the joint-Disney-Seagram project in an observation tower beside the falls" (Pierce, March 20, 2013, n.p.). "It was there that parties discussed Disney's involvement in developing a 'moon trip' attraction on the tower site" (Emerson, 2010, p. 9). Those plans never went anywhere.

Hotel Sheraton Brock

(now the Crowne Plaza Niagara Falls – Fallsview Hotel)
5685 Falls Avenue
Niagara Falls ON Canada L2E 6W7
(905) 374-4447
niagarafallscrowneplazahotel.com

In August 1963, Walt, Lillian, Roy and Edna Disney all traveled on a Beechcraft plane owned by The Walt Disney Company to Niagara Falls (Emerson, 2010). "That evening they joined city officials for dinner at the home of a local business leader, Paul Schoellkopf" (Emerson, 2010, p. 8).

NIAGARA FALLS

☐ **Hotel Sheraton Brock**
☐ **Seagram Tower**

ARRIVED
5 DEC 19...
WALT DISNEY

WALT'S PASSPORT

BRITISH COLUMBIA

Vancouver

W

Food Available	Guided Tour Available	Not Open to the Public	Original Structure Gone	Train Connection	Parking Fee
Post Death Tribute	Hotel	Must See	Multimedia	Admission Fee	Drive By Location

Chapter 69
Vancouver
British Columbia, Canada

The Final Family Vacation: Inlets of British Columbia
In June-July 1966, Walt rented a yacht for the family and they cruised the islands near Vancouver, British Columbia, Canada. Joining Walt and Lillian were: Diane and Ron Miller, Sharon and Robert Brown, and seven grandchildren. They vacationed on this yacht for two weeks (Wednesday with Walt, July 13, 2011).

"'That was sort of a finale for the family in a lot of ways...one of the first pure vacations we had,' Chris [Disney] said...'It was family on an adventure,' Chris continued, 'there wasn't a movie company nearby that grandpa was monitoring and my dad [Ron Miller] wasn't working'" (Holzer, October 12, 2011, n.p.).

Because Walt was working on the CalArts project, he had brought a book on how to choose faculty for colleges to read on vacation (Barrier, 2007).

This vacation took place just five months before Walt died. According to Ron Miller, "I noticed he [Walt] was having a helluva time with his leg. [The pain] came down and it bothered his hip. Whenever he would get in a rowboat or anything, he would have to literally do this to his leg [indicating "lifting" his leg, as though stepping over a low fence]. It was the damnedst thing. And that's as far as the whole family, or anyone, knew was the extent of his illness" (Barrier, 2007, p. 313).

"The grandkids remember fishing and walking through the forests with Walt. Walt loved wearing the captain's hat and leaning on the railing watching the grandkids as they played in the water. During this trip Walt and Lilly celebrated their 41st wedding anniversary, and Tamara celebrated her birthday"

(Titizian, September 21, 2011, n.p.). This trip ended on July 13, 1966 (Barrier, 2007).

MEXICO

Mexico City

Fortín de las Flores

Food Available

Guided Tour Available

Not Open to the Public

Original Structure Gone

Train Connection

Parking Fee

Post Death Tribute

Hotel

Must See

Multimedia

Admission Fee

Drive By Location

Chapter 70
Mexico

Basílica de Guadalupe (Mexico City)
Plaza de las Américas 1
Villa de Guadalupe
Villa Gustavo A. Madero
07050 Ciudad de México
CDMX Mexico

Significance: Walt visited Mexico in these 6 years: 1941, 1942, 1943, 1953, 1954 and 1964 (personal communication, D. Smith, July 5, 2017).

The visits in the 1940s are highlighted.

1941 Visit
As part of the Franklin Delano Roosevelt "Good Neighbor Program," Walt and his colleagues ended a South American journey with a stop in Mexico on their way back to California (Fahr & Seastrom, 2016).

1942 Visit
"Later in 1942, Walt, Mary Blair, and a few others took an additional short research trip to Mexico to gather material for a second film, *The Three Caballeros*, which premiered in Mexico City on December 21, 1944. This film featured the duo of Donald Duck and Brazilian parrot José Carioca from *Saludos Amigos*, and added Mexican charro rooster Panchito. The film showcased live-action highlights from various locations around Mexico, including Acapulco and Veracruz. The Mexican magazine *Tiempo* described Walt as having brought a 'world of friendship and understanding to the people of all countries'"
(Fahr & Seastrom, 2016, n.p.).

"During the production process, Disney traveled to Mexico City in December 1942. He visited schools under the Secretary of Public Education and took a series of cultural outings to locations significant for Mexicans, such as the Basílica de Guadalupe. This...trip helped Mexican teachers meet with the filmmaker and his crew" (Cejudo, 2016, n.p.).

Mexico City

1943 Visit
"On August 30, 1943, Walt received the Order of the Aztec Eagle. This award had only been established a decade before as the highest honor a foreigner could receive from the Mexican government. With co-founder of the MGM Studios, Louis B. Mayer, Walt went along to Mexico City on August 24 to receive their medals directly from Mexican president Manuel Ávila Camacho. The award honored those who have made a great contribution to Mexico, in particular or humankind in general, and focused on Walt's efforts to foster beneficial international relations with Mexico"(Cejudo, 2016, n.p.).

Fortín de las Flores
In the State of Veracruz

"After this Seminar in August and September 1943, Disney and his studio workers traveled for a second time to Mexico and visited the town of Fortín de las Flores in the state of Veracruz. There, Professors Eulalia Guzmán, Guadalupe Cejudo, Estela Soni, and Juan A. Pina took them to visit several classes taught by Pina. The aim was, first, that they would learn about work dynamics in the Mexican schools where educational films were used; second, they would understand the education level of their potential audience; and third, they would hear the opinions of doctors, teachers, and health-care workers on the films' contents during the production process" (Cejudo, 2016, n.p.).

MEXICO

ARRIVED
5 DEC. 1901
WALT DISNEY

- ☐ Basilica de Guadalupe
- ☐ Mexico City
- ☐ Fortin de las Flores

WALT'S PASSPORT

Other Disney Related Locations

Chapter 71
Walt Disney Chapters of DeMolay

For information about DeMolay, see pages 230-231.

Significance: These two chapters honor Walt Disney, who was a member of DeMolay.

Walt Disney Chapter of DeMolay Michigan
106 East Main Street
Northville MI 48167

disneydemolay.org
michigandemolay.com/chapters/walt-disney-chapter
disneydemoly@gmail.com

This chapter is based out of the Northville Lodge No. 186 in Northville, MI in the Northville Masonic Temple building.

Walt Disney Chapter of DeMolay California
303 West Lincoln Avenue
Anaheim CA 92805
(714) 563-1552

DEMOLAY CHAPTERS

ARRIVED
5 DEC 1901
WALT DISNE

☐ **Northville, MI**
☐ **Anaheim, CA**

WALT'S PASSPORT

Chapter 72
Walt Disney Elementary Schools

There are at least 15 known Walt Disney Elementary Schools.

CALIFORNIA
Walt Disney Elementary School (original)
2323 West Orange Avenue
Anaheim CA 92804-3474
magnoliasd.org/schools/walt-disney

Walt Disney Elementary School
3250 Pine Valley Road
San Ramon CA 94583
des.srvusd.k12.ca.us/about

Walt Disney Elementary School
1220 West Orange Grove Avenue
Burbank CA 91506
burbankusd.org/WDE

ILLINOIS
(see pages 193-194 for more information on these 2 schools).

Walt Disney Magnet School
4140 North Marine Drive
Chicago IL 60613
disney.cps.edu

Disney II Magnet Elem. School
3815 North Kedvale Ave
Chicago IL 60641
disneyiimagnet.org

INDIANA
Walt Disney Elementary School
4015 Filbert Road
Mishawaka IN 46545
waltdisney.phmschools.org/

MICHIGAN
Walt Disney Elementary School
36155 Kelly Road
Clinton Township MI 48025
fraser.k12.mi.us/DisneyElementary

MISSOURI
(see page 259-261 for more information)
Walt Disney Elementary
420 East California Avenue
Marceline MO 64658
disney.marcelineschools.org

Walt Disney Elementary School
4100 South Fremont
Springfield MO 65804
disney.spsk12.org/pages/Disney

NEBRASKA
Walt Disney Elementary School
5717 South 112th Street
Omaha NE 68137
disney.mpsomaha.org

NEW YORK
PS 160: The Walt Disney School
4140 Hutchinson River Pkway East
Bronx NY 10475
thewaltdisneyschool.org

Walt Disney Elementary School
175 Coldwater Road
Rochester NY 14624
gateschili.org/disney.cfm?subpage
=3299

OKLAHOMA
Walt Disney Elementary School
11702 East 25th Street
Tulsa OK 74129
disney.tulsa.schooldesk.net/

PENNSYLVANIA
Walt Disney Elementary School
(See page 295 for more
information)
200 Lakeside Drive
Levittown PA 19054
pennsbury.k12.pa.us/pennsbury/Pe
nnsbury/www.pennsbury.k12.pa.us
/pennsbury/Disney/index.html

TEXAS
Walt Disney Elementary School
5000 Mustang Road
Alvin TX 77511
alvinisd.net/Domain/21

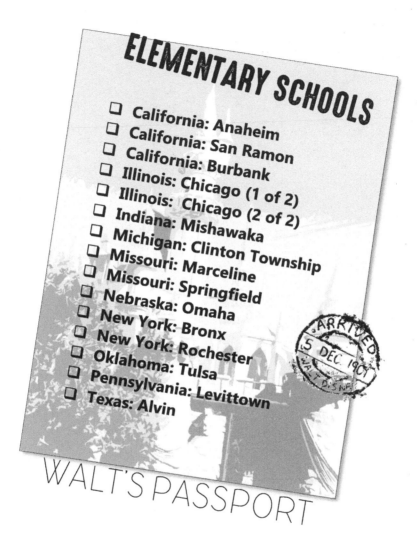

ELEMENTARY SCHOOLS

- ☐ California: Anaheim
- ☐ California: San Ramon
- ☐ California: Burbank
- ☐ Illinois: Chicago (1 of 2)
- ☐ Illinois: Chicago (2 of 2)
- ☐ Indiana: Mishawaka
- ☐ Michigan: Clinton Township
- ☐ Missouri: Marceline
- ☐ Missouri: Springfield
- ☐ Nebraska: Omaha
- ☐ New York: Bronx
- ☐ New York: Rochester
- ☐ Oklahoma: Tulsa
- ☐ Pennsylvania: Levittown
- ☐ Texas: Alvin

ARRIVED
5 DEC 1901
WALT DISNEY

WALT'S PASSPORT

Chapter 73
Other Disney Tributes & Associations

Disney Hall: SUNY Fredonia
Kirkland Complex
State University of New York (SUNY) at Fredonia
Fredonia NY 14063
(716) 673-3111
fredonia.edu
students.fredonia.edu/reslife/disney

Significance: The only known college campus building in the United States bearing Walt Disney's name.

At the State University of New York (SUNY) Fredonia campus, there is a residence hall called "Disney Hall," named after Walt Disney (SUNY, n.d.). This residence hall opened in 1967, one year after the death of Walt Disney (SUNY, n.d.).

In an April 21, 1971 *Jamestown Post-Journal* news article, the Vice President of Student Affairs at the time, Robert E. Coon, stated, "We try to emphasize the individuality of the four separate wings; letting the students name their living units promotes this atmosphere" (personal communication, B. Cummings-Witter, September 5, 2017). Besides, Disney Hall, students also selected these names: Hendrix Hall for Jimi Hendrix, Schultz Hall for Charles Schultz, Hemingway Hall for Ernest Hemingway, Eisenhower Hall for former President Dwight D. Eisenhower, and Grissom Hall for Astronaut Gus Grissom, according to the SUNY Fredonia Library Clerk for Archives and Special Collections.

Online Campus Map:
home.fredonia.edu/maps

Disney Hall is near Temple Street, on the edge of campus.

Silverado Vineyards
6121 Silverado Trail
Napa CA 94558
(855) 270-1770
silveradovineyards.com

Significance: This winery was founded in 1981 by Diane Disney Miller, along with her husband Ron Miller.

"Diane traveled to Napa Valley with her mother, Lillian, to visit several wineries. The trip inspired Miller to start a vineyard, with the possibility of a winery. In 1976, the family purchased a large property along the Silverado Trail in the Stags Leap District. They planted Cabernet Sauvignon and Chardonnay and started making wine in 1981. The early wines were consistently outstanding, with their Limited Reserve Cabernet occasionally rating classic on Wine Spectator's 100-point scale" (Weed, 2013, n.p.).

OTHER AREAS

☐ **SUNY Fredonia: Disney Hall**
☐ **Silverado Vineyards**

ARRIVED
5 DEC 1901
WALT DISNEY

WALT'S PASSPORT

Chapter 74
Walt's Parents Pilgrimage
Elias Disney and Flora (Call) Disney

Alphabetical Order by State

Citronelle, Alabama
When looking to relocate from Chicago, Elias scoped out Citronelle, Alabama, but found it unsuitable and selected Marceline, Missouri (Thomas, 1994; Silvester, 2014). Exact location is unknown.

Anaheim, California
Disneyland
Walt honored Elias Disney with a window on Main Street, U.S.A., on July 17, 1955, the opening day of Disneyland park. It states: "Elias Disney, Contractor, Est. 1895." His honorary window is located above the Emporium.

Disney California Adventure: Elias & Co.
disneyland.disney.go.com/shops/disney-california-adventure/elias-and-co/
A shop on Buena Vista Street named after Walt's father, Elias Disney.

Glendale, California
Between 1920 and 1921 in Glendale, California, Elias helped one of Flora's relatives build a house (Thomas, 1994). According to Thomas (1998), Elias only spent $1 during the 3 months he stayed there.

Walt used to take Elias and Flora on a drive and they would request to visit Forest Lawn Cemetery. According to Walt, "I left them at the gate, and they would walk around all afternoon. Then I'd pick them up toward evening" (Thomas, 1998, p. 146). [Walt] "said they both drew inspiration from the cemetery, with its wide hilly lawns dotted with reproductions of classic sculpture" (Thomas, 1998, p. 146).

Elias and Flora Call are both buried in the Forest Lawn Cemetery in Glendale. (see pages 51-52 for more information).

Los Angeles, California

On January 1, 1938, Elias and Flora Disney celebrated their 50th wedding anniversary at Walt's home on Woking Way (see pages 70-71 for more information). All five of the Disney children were present (Watts, 1997). "Walt, ever the showman and historian, tape-recorded much of the event. Conducting a mock interview with his parents, he joked that his notoriously strict father "always enjoyed a good time" and inquired playfully, 'Don't you want to make whoopee on your golden wedding anniversary?' The slightly nonplussed Elias replied, 'Oh, we don't want to go to any extremes a-tall' as Flora added, 'He don't know how to make whoopee" (Watts, 1997, p. 16).

In Los Angeles, Elias discovered that he was never an American citizen. He had been voting illegally for 50 years. Elias took care of that at the federal building to resolve this issue (Thomas, 1998).

 View Elias and Flora Disney in this video clip (no audio): Search "So Dear To My Heart: Elias and Flora" on YouTube.

Steamboat Springs, Colorado

When looking to relocate from Chicago, Elias scoped out Steamboat Springs, Colorado, but found it unsuitable and selected Marceline, Missouri (Thomas, 1994; Silvester, 2014).

Denver, Colorado

Elias took a job as a machinist in a railroad shop, which brought him to Denver, where his position as an apprentice carpenter finished. Elias attempted to make money playing his fiddle with two other musicians at outside saloons, but that was not successful so he returned to Ellis, Kansas (Thomas, 1994).

Acron, Florida

"Acron was a town in eastern Lake County, Florida, established during the late 19th century, near Paisley. It is best known as the town where Flora Call and Elias Disney...and Roy O. Disney lived for a short time after they were married" (Acron, n.d., n.p.).

Daytona Beach, Florida

Elias and Flora "actually lived for a time beginning that year in Daytona Beach; their first son (Herbert Arthur Disney) was born there in December 1888. For a short time, Elias operated and lived in Daytona Beach's Halifax Hotel... Halifax Avenue was, and is, a major thoroughfare in Daytona Beach" (Smith, n.d.). But that business venture was unsuccessful as tourism dropped and Elias went out of business (Thomas, 1994).

According to the Walt Disney Birthplace website, the Halifax Hotel was "one of Daytona Beach's first tourist lodgings" (Walt Disney Birthplace, December 17, 2013, n.p.). It seems like the Halifax Hotel no longer exists.

Elias then worked as a rural mailman and purchased a small orange grove (Thomas, 1994).

Elias enlisted in the militia for a short while. Military police tried to arrest him for disserting the militia but Elias was never arrested (Thomas, 1994).

Later, a frost destroyed Elias' orange crop and then he came down with malaria (Thomas, 1994). That's when the Disney family moved to Chicago (Thomas, 1994).

Kismet, Florida

Elias and his father visited the Call family in Florida. Kepple returned to Ellis, Kansas, but Elias stayed. Elias purchased a farm of 40 acres and courted Flora Call, who was a school teacher in the area (Thomas, 1994).

Kismet is where Elias and Flora were married on New Year's Day in 1888 (Thomas, 1994). Elias was 28 and Flora was 19 (Thomas, 1994).

After they were married, Elias sold that farm and purchased a hotel in Daytona Beach, Florida (Thomas, 1994).

Kissimmee, Florida

Elias worked for a short time as a mailman here (Elias Disney, n.d.).

Lake Buena Vista, Florida

Walt Disney World Resort: Magic Kingdom
Elias Disney also has a window on Main Street, U.S.A. It is on Center Street above the Uptown Jewelers.

Tampa, Florida

Just outside of Tampa is where Elias spent his time in basic training in a boot camp with the militia (Silvester, 2014).

Chicago, Illinois

Where Elias, Flora and Herbert relocated to after leaving Florida in 1889 (Thomas, 1994).

"By 1890, the Disneys lived at 3515 South Vernon Avenue in the Fourth Ward" (Elias Disney, n.d., n.p.).

Flora did the floor plans for a house and Elias built a small house at 1249 Tripp Avenue in Chicago (Thomas, 1994). Tripp Avenue was one of two paved roads in that part of northwestern Chicago at the time (Thomas, 1994).

Elias worked as a carpenter at the 1893 World's Columbia Exposition in Chicago (Thomas, 1994).

Here, four more Disney family members were born: Raymond Arnold Disney (December 30, 1890), Roy Oliver Disney (June 24, 1893), Walter Elias Disney (December 5, 1901), and Ruth Flora Disney (December 6, 1903) (Thomas, 1994).

The Disney family attended services at St. Paul Congregational Church (Thomas, 1994). (See page 186 for more information on the church). Elias helped build the church and Flora played the organ. Elias provided the sermons when preacher Walter Parr was on vacation (Thomas, 1994).

The Disney family returned to Chicago in 1917. Elias reluctantly paid for Walt's art courses as long as Walt contributed to the family income (Thomas, 1994).

In Chicago, Elias refused to sign Walt's application for a passport so Walt could join the American Ambulance Corps. So Flora forged his name on the application (Thomas, 1994).

In 1920, Elias lost his investment in the O-Zell jelly factory when it went bankrupt (Thomas, 1994). Elias and Flora departed Chicago and returned to Kansas City.

Ellis, Kansas
In 1878, Elias' father, Kepple Disney, set off for the California gold fields with Elias and Elias' brother, Robert. They did not reach California as Kepple stopped near Ellis, Kansas and purchased 200 acres of Union Pacific land (Thomas, 1994). Kepple sent for the rest of the family and built a house made of sod (Thomas, 1994).

Elias "became restless on the farm and left for a job as machinist in a railroad shop, where a co-worker was Walter Chrysler, founder of the automotive empire" (Thomas, 1994, p. 22). (See pages 199-200 for more information on Ellis, Kansas and the Walter Chrysler Museum).

Elias returned to the family after a short stint in Denver, Colorado (see pages 350-351).

The Call family lived in Ellis, Kansas. Charles Call had left Oberlin College to seek gold in California, but found no gold. He then moved his family (8 daughters and 2 sons) to Ellis. Charles taught school. According to Thomas, "the prairie blizzards convinced Charles Call to move his family to Florida in 1884" (1994, p. 22).

Kansas City, Missouri
In Spring 1910, the Disney family moved to Kansas City.

In September, 1914, Elias purchased a home on Bellefontaine Street (Elias Disney, n.d.) (for more information, see page 232).

At age 51, Elias purchased a paper route and also added a new kitchen, bathroom and bedroom to the home (Thomas, 1994).

In 1920, Elias and Flora returned to Kansas City from Chicago. They still owned the house on Bellefontaine. Elias charged Walt $5 a month to use the garage for his animation work (Thomas, 1994).

According to Thomas (1998), while in Kansas City, Elias was known to carry a little old pocket book that contained one quarter. Flora would often replace the quarter because the last one was turning green.

Marceline, Missouri

Elias moved his family here in April 1906 because Elias's brother, Robert, owned property here (Thomas, 1994). "Elias Disney decided Marceline would be the place where he could earn a good living and rear his five children in a wholesome Christian atmosphere" (Thomas, 1994, p. 25).

According to Bob Thomas (1998), Elias and Flora rarely attended church in Marceline because there was not a Congregationalist church there.

"In 1907, Elias convinced some of his fellow farmers to join the American Society of Equity, a farmer's union aiming to consolidate the members' buying power" (Elias Disney, n.d.).

In Winter 1909, Elias contracted typhoid fever followed by pneumonia (Thomas, 1994). As a result, the family sold the farm on November 28, 1910 in Marceline and moved to Kansas City, Missouri (Thomas, 1994; Elias Disney, n.d.).

In 1917, Elias grew restless since the newspaper route had not grown. So he invested $16,000 in the O-Zell jelly factory in Chicago and moved back there (Thomas, 1994).

(For more information on Marceline, see Chapter 53).

St. Louis, Missouri

In 1934, Flora and Elias Disney took a trip to St. Louis (no other details are known) (Madden, 2017).

Steuben, Ohio

Birthplace of Flora Call Disney, Walt's mother (see Chapter 57)
1860 Greenfield
Steuben OH 44890

Portland, Oregon
1630 Southeast Morrison Street
Portland OR 97214

Elias and Flora moved here from Kansas City in the Fall of 1921, primarily because their son Herbert had been transferred here by the United States Postal Service (Winton, 2015; Thomas, 1994). Walt and Lillian visited Elias and Flora Disney (Walt's parents) in Portland in the summer of 1925, after their honeymoon at Mt. Rainier National Park and Seattle, Washington (Gabler, 2006).

Bluevale/Wingham, Ontario, Canada
This is the birthplace of Elias Disney.
For more information about this site, see page 319-320.

ELIAS & FLORA PILGRIMAGE

- ☐ Alabama
- ☐ Anaheim, CA: Disneyland
- ☐ Anaheim, CA: Disney California Adventure
- ☐ Glendale, CA
- ☐ Los Angeles, CA
- ☐ Colorado
- ☐ Denver, CO
- ☐ Acron, FL
- ☐ Daytona Beach, FL
- ☐ Kismet, FL
- ☐ Kissimmee, FL
- ☐ Lake Buena Vista, FL
- ☐ Chicago, IL
- ☐ Ellis, KS
- ☐ Kansas City, MO
- ☐ Marceline, MO
- ☐ Steuben, OH
- ☐ Portland, OR
- ☐ Ontario, Canada

ARRIVED
5 DEC. 1901
WALT DISNE.

WALT'S PASSPORT

Appendix

Other Resources and Opportunities

Walt Disney's Hollywood

cdn.media.d23.com/html/waltshollywood/html/index.html
By D23 (Official Disney Fan Club)
(See page 361 for more information.)

"Take a virtual walk in Walt Disney's footsteps through many of the old Hollywood haunts where the great man worked, lived and, played!"

The Walt Disney Guide to Los Angeles

la.curbed.com/maps/walt-disney-map

An online map of 5 major destinations hosted by Curbed LA

Finding Walt Website

Findingwalt.com

This website features a directory of important places in Walt's life. It includes an interactive Google Map.

There is also a facebook page for Finding Walt:
facebook.com/FindingWalt

Zip-A-Dee-Doo-Pod Cast

Episode 72
ZADDP #72: The Walt Disney Pilgrimage
August 4, 2015
By Aaron Wallace

ottoradio.com/podcast/120896549/120896549-2?place=discovery
Start the podcast at 14:15.

Waltland: Disney History Bus Tour
waltland.com

This site and tour is hosted by Bob Gurr, Disney Legend and former Disney Imagineer. Periodic tours are offered. The tour highlights 15 places, including stops at 8 locations: Walt's homes, Hyperion Studios site, Griffith Park Merry-Go-Round, the Walt Disney Barn Museum, MAPO, Walt Disney Imagineering, Grand Central Air Terminal, and Walt Disney Studios.

D23 Official Disney Fan Club: Special Events
d23.com

Membership Fee Required:
d23.com/membership-information

Events:	d23.com/d23-events
D23 Expo (every 2 years):	d23.com/d23-expo

Previous member-only events have included: a visit to the Walt Disney Birthplace in Chicago, a tour of Walt Disney's Office Suite at the Studios in Burbank, and a Walt Disney Studios tour.

Walt Disney's Progressland
Smithsonian Institution Archives
https://siarchives.si.edu/blog/walt-disney-progressland

Tour of the Walt Disney Studios Lot
babble.com/disney/take-a-tour-of-the-walt-disney-studios-lot/

Adventures by Disney

(owned and operated by The Walt Disney Company)
Disneyland Resort and Southern California Tour
adventuresbydisney.com/north-america/hollywood-disneyland-tour/

Includes: Lunch at the Tam O'Shanter, The Walt Disney
Studios, The Walt Disney Archives, VIP Visit to
Disneyland (and lots of other non-Walt Disney related
activities).

Prices start at $2,899 for adults.

The Disneyland Gazette Podcast

Episode 141: The Walt Pilgrimage
October 1, 2012

disneylandgazette.com/the-disneyland-gazette---issue-141-
(10112).html
Start the podcast at 24:00.

▶ Biographical Movies about Walt Disney

As Dreamers Do   waltmovie.com

PBS Documentary
pbs.org/wgbh/americanexperience/films/walt-disney

Saving Mr. Banks   movies.disney.com/saving-mr-banks

Walt Before Mickey   waltbeforemickey.com

Walt: The Man Behind the Myth
store.wdfmuseum.org/walt-the-man-behind-the-myth-dvd-blu-ray

References

21 Royal. (n.d.). Retrieved from 21royaldisneyland.com

100 S. Orange Avenue. (2017). Loopnet. Retrieved from
http://www.loopnet.com/Listing/17410624/100-S-ORANGE-AVENUE-Orlando-FL/

1960 Winter Olympics. (2017). Wikipedia entry. Retrieved from
en.wikipedia.org/wiki/1960_Winter_Olympics

2719 Hyperion (June 29, 2015). Walt Disney's Los Angeles: Los Feliz 2015. Retrieved from
http://2719hyperion.blogspot.com/search/label/Disney's Hollywood

Acron, Florida. Retrieved from https://en.wikipedia.org/wiki/Acron,_Florida

Anderson, P. (July 19, 2011). Walt Disney The Golfer, Swope Park, Kansas City. Retrieved from
disneyhistoryinstitute.com/2011/07/walt-disney-golf-swope-park-kansas-city.html

Anderson, P. (March 17, 2010). Walt's People-Joyce C. Hall. Retrieved from
disneyhistoryinstitute.com/2010/03/walts-people-joyce-c-hall.html

Apgar, G. (April 6, 2016). It's a Small World: Disney in Connecticut. *Connecticut Magazine*. Retrieved
from http://www.connecticutmag.com/the-connecticut-story/it-s-a-small-world-disney-in-
connecticut/article_13c50a0f-8a76-5589-b3d8-4a24d752d6f5.html

Art Institute of Chicago. (n.d). Thorne Miniature Rooms. Retrieved from
http://www.artic.edu/aic/collections/thorne

Arthur, A. (January 5, 2006). When the Desert Was Disney's Land. *Palm Springs Life*. Retrieved from
http://www.palmspringslife.com/when-the-desert-was-disneys-land/

Babbitt, A. (April 11, 2012). The Snow White Wrap Party – part 1. *BabbittBlog: The Official Blog of an
Animation Legend*. Retrieved from https://babbittblog.com/2012/04/11/the-snow-white-wrap-party-
part-1/

Baham, J. (August 28, 2017). Mousetalgia Podcast 462: A chat with Rolly Crump; inside Disneyland's
21 Royal. Retrieved from http://micechat.com/169774-mousetalgia-podcast-462-chat-rolly-crump-
inside-disneylands-21-royal

Barnes, B. (March 31, 2009). *Museum Is to Show the Human Side of a Cartoon Titan*. Retrieved from
http://www.nytimes.com/2009/04/01/movies/01disn.html?mcubz=3

Barrier, M. (2007). *An Animated Man*. University of California Press.

Barrier, M. (2015). Walt's Adventures in the Ivy League. Retrieved from
http://www.michaelbarrier.com/Essays/WaltAtHarvard/WaltAtHarvard.html

Bay Lake, Florida. Retrieved from https://en.wikipedia.org/wiki/Bay_Lake,_Florida

Belobradic, M. (April 22, 2017). Walt Disney's Canadian Roots: The Disney Family Tree in Canada. 1923
Main Street. Retrieved from http://www.1923mainstreet.com/roots.html

Bergen, E. (May 8, 2015). The Walt Disney Stamp of 1968. Yesterland. Retrieved from
http://www.yesterland.com/wdstamp.html.

Bohemian Grove (n.d.). Retrieved from https://en.wikipedia.org/wiki/Bohemian_Grove

Brennan, M. (June 9, 2013). Exclusive: The $90 Million Carolwood Estate Once Owned by Walt Disney. *Forbes.* Retrieved from https://www.forbes.com/sites/morganbrennan/2013/06/09/exclusive-the-90-million-carolwood-estate-once-owned-by-walt-disney/#281cbcd5cd47

Brock, B.B. (n.d.). Walt Disney's Palm Springs home. Finding Walt. Retrieved from http://www.findingwalt.com/walt-disneys-palm-springs-home

Built, D. (2017). *Colony Plaza Hotel.* Abandoned Florida. Retrieved from http://www.abandonedfl.com/colony-plaza-hotel/

Burnes, B., Butler, R.W. & D. Viets, (2002). *Walt Disney's Missouri.* Kansas City Star Books: Kansas City.

CalArts (n.d.). Chouinard Art Institute. Retrieved from https://calarts.edu/about/institute/history/chouinard-art-institute

CalArts (n.d.b). Timeline. Retrieved from https://calarts.edu/about/institute/history/timeline

CalArts School of Dance. (n.d.). Facilities. Retrieved from https://dance.calarts.edu/facilities

CalArts School of Music. (n.d.). Facilities. Retrieved from https://music.calarts.edu/facilities.

California Hall of Fame (2017). Overview. Retrieved from californiamuseum.org/california-hall-fame

Carnaham, A. (June 26, 2012). Look Closer: 1964 New York World's Fair. Retrieved from http://waltdisney.org/blog/look-closer-1964-new-york-world%E2%80%99s-fair

Carolwood Foundation (n.d.a). Calendar. Retrieved from http://carolwood.com/calendar.

Carolwood Foundation (n.d.b). Walt's Barn. Retrieved from carolwood.com/walts-barn

Cejudo, M. (July 2016). Disney Health Films in Mexico. Retrieved from http://latinamericanhistory.oxfordre.com/view/10.1093/acrefore/9780199366439.001.0001/acrefore-9780199366439-e-318#ref_acrefore-9780199366439-e-318-note-6

Center for Early Childhood Creativity and Innovation (CECCI). (n.d.). Retrieved from cecciwdb.org

Chasen's (n.d.). Retrieved from https://en.wikipedia.org/wiki/Chasen%27s

Children's Fairyland. (2016). History of the Park. Retrieved from http://fairyland.org/all-about-fairyland/park-attractions/

City of Garden Grove (n.d.). *Disney Garage Studio.* Retrieved from ci.garden-grove.ca.us//HistoricalSociety/disney

Colony Theater. (n.d.). Retrieved from http://www.nycago.org/Organs/NYC/html/ColonyTheater.html

Crawford, H. (April 30, 2010). *Walt Disney – King of Fantasy.* Palm Springs Life (Reprinted from the July 1965 Issue of Palm Springs Life magazine.) Retrieved from http://www.palmspringslife.com/walt-disney-king-of-fantasy/

Cruise, G. (June 24, 2012). Walt Disney-The Canadian Connection. Retrieved from http://land.allears.net/blogs/guestblog/2012/06/walt_disney_the_canadian_conne_1.html

D23 Disney Fan Club (n.d.a). Dave Smith, Disney Legend. Retrieved from https://d23.com/walt-disney-legend/dave-smith/

D23 Disney Fan Club (n.d.b). Walt Disney Quotes. Retrieved from https://d23.com/walt-disney-quote/page/3/

D23 Disney Fan Club (n.d.c). Disney Legends. Retrieved from https://d23.com/disney-legends/

D23 Disney Fan Club (n.d.d). Walt Disney Receives First Honorary Degree. Retrieved from https://d23.com/this-day/walt-disney-receives-first-honorary-degree/

D23 Disney Fan Club (n.d.e). Walt's Hidden Hideaway: Smoke Tree Ranch. Retrieved from https://d23.com/walts-hidden-hideaway/)

D23 Disney Fan Club (December 7, 2015). *Walt Disney's Office Suite Restored as Permanent Exhibit Space*. Retrieved from https://d23.com/walt-disneys-office-suite-restored-as-permanent-exhibit-space/

D23 Disney Fan Club (March 7, 2016). D23 Takes the First Tour of the Walt Disney Birthplace. Retrieved from https://d23.com/d23-event-recaps/event-recap-d23-presents-walt-disneys-chicago/

Discover Los Angeles (April 27, 2017). The Top 10 Must Sees and Hidden Gems at the Walt Disney Concert Hall. Retrieved from http://www.discoverlosangeles.com/blog/top-10-must-sees-hidden-gems-walt-disney-concert-hall

Disney Avenue (December 31, 2016). *Forever Remembered: The Lasting Influence of Walt Disney*. Retrieved from http://www.disneyavenue.com/2016/12/forever-remembered-lasting-influence-of.html

Disney II Magnet (n.d.). Mission/Vision: History. Retrieved from http://disneyiimagnet.org/apps/pages/index.jsp?uREC_ID=199311&type=d&termREC_ID=&pREC_ID=398995

Disney Wiki (n.d.a). Hollywood Walk of Fame. Retrieved from: http://disney.wikia.com/wiki/Hollywood_Walk_of_Fame

Disney Wiki (n.d.b). California Institute of Arts. Retrieved from http://disney.wikia.com/wiki/California_Institute_of_the_Arts

Disneyland. (n.d.a). "Walk in Walt's Disneyland Footsteps" Guided Tour. Retrieved from https://disneyland.disney.go.com/events-tours/disneyland/walk-in-walts-disneyland-footsteps/

Disneyland. (n.d.b). Enhanced Tiki Room. Retrieved from https://disneyland.disney.go.com/attractions/disneyland/enchanted-tiki-room/

Disneyland Resort (2017). *The Disneyland Story presenting Great Moments with Mr. Lincoln*. Retrieved from https://disneyland.disney.go.com/attractions/disneyland/disneyland-story/

Doyle, G. (November 17, 2014). Confirmed: Disneyland's Lilly Belle car Now Open Once More. Daily Dose. Retrieved from http://disneydose.com/disneyland-lilly-belle-car-closed/#axzz4kZumu6B7

Eisterhold Associates, Inc. (2001). *Tour Guide of Marceline, Missouri: Walt Disney's Home Town.*

Elias Disney. Retrieved from https://en.wikipedia.org/wiki/Elias_Disney

Emerson, C. (2010). *Project Future: The Inside Story Behind the Creation of Disney World.* Ayefour Publishing.

Fahr, T. & L.O. Seastrom. (August 26, 2016). Walt and Mexico—An Honored Friendship. Retrieved from http://waltdisney.org/blog/walt-and-mexico-honored-friendship

Fickley-Baker, J. (August 11, 2017). *Star Wars*: Galaxy's Edge & Toy Story Land Models on Display Soon at Disney's Hollywood Studios. Retrieved from https://disneyparks.disney.go.com/blog/2017/08/star-wars-galaxys-edge-toy-story-land-models-on-display-soon-at-disneys-hollywood-studios/?CMP=SOC-DPFY17Q4DPBSupport0010A

Findagrave.com. (October 4, 2011). Eber Call. Retrieved from https://www.findagrave.com/cgi-bin/fg.cgi?page=gr&GRid=77617228

Findingwalt.com (n.d.). Walt Disney's Los Feliz home. Retrieved from http://www.findingwalt.com/walt-disneys-los-feliz-home/)

Findthecompany.com (2017). The Walt and Lilly Disney Foundation. Retrieved from http://nonprofits.findthecompany.com/l/915372/The-Walt-and-Lilly-Disney-Foundation

Findingmickey.com (n.d.). Walt Disney's Griffith Park Bench. Retrieved from http://findingmickey.squarespace.com/disneyland-facts/main-street-usa/3569479

Flora Call Disney. Retrieved from https://en.wikipedia.org/wiki/Flora_Call_Disney

Frevele, J. (January 22, 2015). The Communist Connection Between Walt Disney and Ronald Reagan. Uproxx. Retrieved from http://uproxx.com/movies/david-henrie-reagan/

Gabler, N. (2006). *Walt Disney: The Biography*. Aurum Press: United Kingdom.

Gabler, N. (December 3, 2006). 'Walt Disney' (First Chapter). *New York Times*. Retrieved from http://www.nytimes.com/2006/12/03/books/chapters/1203-1st-gabl.html

Garland, C. (December 24, 2015). *Walt Disney's Burbank office suite restored to historic glory*. Retrieved from http://www.latimes.com/socal/burbank-leader/news/tn-blr-walt-disneys-burbank-office-suite-restored-to-historic-glory-20151224-story.html.

Gilmore Car Museum. (2016). Disney Magic and More. In Gilmore Car Museum. Retrieved July 11, 2016, from gilmorecarmuseum.org/visit-explore-2/must-sees/disney-magic-more

Gilmore Stadium (n.d.). Retrieved from https://en.wikipedia.org/wiki/Gilmore_Stadium

Glover, E. (May 4, 2012). A Look Inside the Exclusive 1901 in Carthay Circle Theatre at Disney California Adventure Park. Retrieved from https://disneyparks.disney.go.com/blog/2012/05/a-look-inside-the-exclusive-1901-in-carthay-circle-theatre-at-disney-california-adventure-park/

Glover, E. (December 21, 2011). Opening Night, 1937: 'Snow White and the Seven Dwarfs' Premieres at Carthay Circle Theatre. *Disneyland Resort, Disney Parks Blog*. Retrieved from http://laist.com/2009/01/31/laistory_carthay_circle_theater.php

Glover, E. (August 18, 2011). Inside Club 33 at Disneyland Park. Disney Parks Blog. Retrieved from https://disneyparks.disney.go.com/blog/2011/08/inside-club-33-at-disneyland-park/

Golden Oak Ranch. (n.d.). History. Retrieved from goldenoakranch.com/about/history/

Great Ideas Creative Group (2015). Disney Legends Ceremony. Retrieved from http://greatideascreativegroup.com/portfolio/disney-legends-ceremony/

Green, R. (Summer 2014). The Roots of Animation in Kansas City. *Jackson County Historical Society Journal*. Retrieved from http://jchs.org/summer2014/

Greenfield Village Visit. (n.d.). Retrieved from d23.com/this-day/walt-returns-to-the-studio-after-10day-trip-to-chicago-and-greenfield-village/

Hall of Famous Missourians. (n.d.). Walter Elias Disney (1901-1966). Retrieved from house.mo.gov/famous.aspx?fm=14

Hallmark Visitor's Center. (2017). Disney. Retrieved from hallmarkvisitorscenter.com/what-youll-see/Detail/Disney

Harvard-Westlake School (n.d.). Retrieved from https://en.wikipedia.org/wiki/Harvard-Westlake_School

Hollywood Walk of Fame (HWOF) (n.d.). Hollywood Walk of Fame. Retrieved from http://www.walkoffame.com/pages/history

Holmby Hills (2017). *History.* Retrieved from: http://www.hw.com/about/History

Holmby Hills, Los Angeles. (n.d.). Retrieved from htttps://en.wikipedia.org/wiki/Holmby_Hills,_Los_Angeles

Holzer, L. (October 12, 2011). "He was always grandpa": The Miller children recall Walt Disney. Retrieved from http://jimhillmedia.com/guest_writers1/b/leo_n_holzer/archive/2011/10/12/quot-he-was-always-grandpa-quot-the-miller-children-recall-walt-disney.aspx

Jackson, K.M. (November 30, 2005). *Walt Disney: Conversations.* University of Mississippi Press.

JustDisney.com (2017). 45 Years of Magic. Retrieved from justdisney.com/Features/disneyland_magic/45_years_of_magic

Kalamazoo Art Center (1959-1965). (n.d.). Information PDF. Retrieved from http://www.wou.edu/wp/exhibits/files/2015/07/Kalamazoo-Art.pdf

Kansas City Art Institute (KCAI). (n.d.). Timeline of the Kansas City Art Institute. Retrieved from http://kcai.edu/about/history/kcai-timeline

WESH2. (December 10, 2014). 5 Facts about Disney's Partner Statue. Retrieved from http://www.wesh.com/article/5-facts-about-disney-s-partners-statue/4330719

Korkis, J. (September 20, 2017). Debunking Myths about Walt Disney. Retrieved from https://www.mouseplanet.com/11885/Debunking_Myths_About_Walt_Disney

Korkis, J. (June 14, 2017). *Walt's Canadian Connections.* MousePlanet. Retrieved from https://www.mouseplanet.com/11799/Walts_Canadian_Connections

Korkis, J. (2016). *How to be a Disney Historian.* Theme Park Press.

Korkis, J. (December 21, 2016). Twelve Stories of Disneyland: Part Two. MousePlanet. Retrieved from https://www.mouseplanet.com/11642/Twelve_Stories_of_Disneyland_Part_Two

Korkis, J. (May 11, 2016). The Story of the Upjohn Pharmacy at Disneyland. Retrieved from https://www.mouseplanet.com/11400/The_Story_of_the_Upjohn_Pharmacy_at_Disneyland

Korkis, J. (2015). *The Vault of Walt: Volume 4.* Theme Park Press.

Korkis, J. (September 10, 2014). *The Importance of the 1948 Chicago Railroad Fair.* MousePlanet. Retrieved from mouseplanet.com/10796/The_Importance_of_the_1948_Chicago_Railroad_Fair

Korkis, J. (April 17, 2013). The Harvard-Disney Connections. Retrieved from https://www.mouseplanet.com/10280/The_HarvardDisney_Connections

Korkis, J. (October 26, 2011). The History of the Partners Statue: Part One (MousePlanet). Retrieved from https://www.mouseplanet.com/9766/The_History_of_the_Partners_Statue_Part_One

Korkis, J. (February 16, 2011). *Remembering Bill Justice*. MousePlanet. Retrieved from https://www.mouseplanet.com/9540/Remembering_Bill_Justice

Kurtti, J. (n.d.). The Wonderful World of WALT: Aloha and Mahalo, Walt Disney. Oh My Disney. Retrieved from https://ohmy.disney.com/insider/2012/07/16/the-wonderful-world-of-walt-aloha-and-mahalo/

Lebo, J. (October 21, 2010). Looking Back: Remembering when Walt Disney came to Levittown. Bucks Local News. Retrieved from: http://www.buckslocalnews.com/bristol_pilot/looking-back-remembering-when-walt-disney-came-to-levittown/article_02b544b9-3590-520c-b439-8de97df55299.html

Lesjak, D. (2015). *In the Service of the Red Cross*. Theme Park Press.

Liberty, J. (2014, August 2). Walt Disney in Kalamazoo: Filmmaker's visit among milestones at Gilmore Car Museum. Kalamazoo Gazette. Retrieved from mlive.com/entertainment/kalamazoo/index.ssf/2014/08/walt_disney_in_kalamazoo_filmm.html

Living in Kalamazoo. (n.d.). Retrieved from http://www.kalamazoomi.com/hisf.htm

Los Angeles Conservancy. (January 17, 2017). Charlotte and Robert Disney House. https://www.laconservancy.org/issues/charlotte-and-robert-disney-house

Los Angeles Conservancy. (2016). Charlotte and Robert Disney House. Retrieved from https://www.laconservancy.org/locations/charlotte-and-robert-disney-house

Los Angeles Department of Recreation and Parks (n.d.). Griffith Park Merry-Go-Round. Retrieved from laparks.org/griffithpark/griffith-park-merry-go-round

Los Angeles Philharmonic (2017). About the Walt Disney Concert Hall. Retrieved from http://www.laphil.com/philpedia/about-walt-disney-concert-hall

Los Angeles Times. (November 27, 1938). Gas Fumes Kill Disney's Mother.

Louis Grell Foundation. (September 21, 2013). What is the connection between Louis Grell and Walt Disney? Retrieved from http://www.louisgrell.com/2013/09/21/a-connection-between-louis-grell-and-walt-disney/

Lt. Robin Crusoe, U.S.N. (n.d.). Retrieved from https://en.wikipedia.org/wiki/Lt._Robin_Crusoe,_U.S.N.

Madden, S.M. (2017). *The Sorcerer's Brother: How Roy O. Disney Made Walt's Magic Possible*. Theme Park Press.

Mahne, Keith. (2015, April 29). The Story Behind the Florida Press Conference. Retrieved from: http://www.disneyavenue.com/2015/04/the-story-behind-florida-press-confrence.html

Marlborough School (n.d.). History and Tradition. Retrieved from https://www.marlborough.org/about/history-tradition

Mathers, S. (April 14, 2005). Ocoee Wants an Overhaul. *Orlando Sentinel.* Retrieved from http://articles.orlandosentinel.com/2005-04-14/news/0504130561_1_ocoee-walt-disney-town-center

Miller, D.D. (1956). *The Story of Walt Disney: A fabulous rags-to-riches saga.* Dell Publishing Co., Inc.: New York.

Missouri Revised Statutes (August 28, 2016). Section 9.220.1: October 16, Walt Disney—'A Day to Dream' Day. Retrieved from moga.mo.gov/mostatutes/stathtml/00900002201.html

Mosley, L. (1992). *Disney's World*. Scarborough House: Lanham, MD.

Municipality of Morris-Turnberry (2012). *A Harvest of Memories (Volume I and II)*. Pinpoint Publications Limited: London, ON, Canada.

National Park Service. (April 24, 2017). Places to Go: Sequoia and Kings Canyon. Retrieved from https://www.nps.gov/seki/planyourvisit/placestogo.htm

New York City Parks. (n.d.). Flushing Meadows Corona Park World's Fair Legacy. Retrieved from https://www.nycgovparks.org/highlights/fmcp-worlds-fairs/virtual-video-tour

The Norconian Resort Supreme (n.d.). Retrieved from https://en.wikipedia.org/wiki/The_Norconian_Resort_Supreme

Northwest Arctic Borough (2017). Retrieved from https://en.wikipedia.org/wiki/Northwest_Arctic_Borough,_Alaska

Palm Springs Homes and Condos for Sale. (July 12, 2010). You Can Live in Walt Disney's Former Palm Springs Smoke Tree Ranch Neighborhood. Retrieved from palmspringshomesandcondosforsale.com /2010/07/12/live-in-walt-disneys-former-palm-springs-smoke-tree-ranch-neighborhood/

Parker, A. (April 15, 2017). *Secret Canadians*. Blogs: Nosey Parker. TorontoSun.com. Retrieved from http://blogs.canoe.com/parker/news/secret-canadians/

Pierce. T.J. (September 16, 2013). Walt's Field Day – 1938. *Disney History Institute*. Retrieved from http://www.disneyhistoryinstitute.com/2013/09/walts-field-day-1938.html

Pierce, T.J. (April 29, 2013). Walt Disney and Riverfront Square Part 9. Retrieved from http://www.disneyhistoryinstitute.com/2013/04/walt-disney-and-riverfront-square-part-9.html

Pierce, T.J. (April 22, 2013). Walt Disney and Riverfront Square Part 8. Retrieved from http://www.disneyhistoryinstitute.com/2013/04/walt-disney-and-riverfront-square-part-8.html

Pierce, T.J. (March 25, 2013). Walt Disney and Riverfront Square – Part 4. Retrieved from http://www.disneyhistoryinstitute.com/2013/03/walt-disney-and-riverfront-square-part-4.html

Pierce, T.J. (March 20, 2013). Walt Disney and Riverfront Square – Part 2. Retrieved from http://www.disneyhistoryinstitute.com/2013/03/walt-disney-and-riverfront-square-part-2.html

Playland (2017). Playland FAQs. Retrieved from http://www.playland-not-at-the-beach.org/faqs_01.html#what

Post Cereals. (n.d.). Wikipedia entry. Retrieved from en.wikipedia.org/wiki/Post_Cereals

Proclamation 5585 – Walt Disney Recognition Day, 1986 (n.d.). Findingwalt.com. Retrieved from http://www.findingwalt.com/waltdisneyday/

Radish, C. (September 24, 2014). *10 Things to Know about Walt Disney's Beloved Home at Woking Way*. Retrieved from http://collider.com/walt-disney-woking-way-home-images/

Red Car Trolley News Boys. (2017). *Disneyland Resort*. Retrieved from https://disneyland.disney.go.com/entertainment/disney-california-adventure/red-car-trolley-news-boys/

REDCAT. (2016). CalArts Connection. Retrieved from https://www.redcat.org/about/calarts-connection

Reedy Creek Improvement District (RCID). (2016a). Homepage. Retrieved from https://www.rcid.org/

Reedy Creek Improvement District (RCID). (2016b). About. Retrieved from https://www.rcid.org/about

Reedy Creek Improvement District (RCID). (n.d.). Retrieved from https://sites.google.com/site/theoriginalepcot/the-reedy-creek-improvement-district

Regan, P. (2009). *Hallmark: A Century of Caring*. Andrews McMeel Publishing, LLC.

Rivera, H.H. (October 22, 2009). Did You Miss It? The Disneyland Attraction That's Millions of Years Old. Retrieved from https://disneyparks.disney.go.com/blog/2009/10/did-you-miss-it-the-disneyland-attraction-that%E2%80%99s-millions-of-years-old/

Roy and Edna CalArts Theatre (REDCAT). (2016). About REDCAT. Retrieved from https://www.redcat.org/about

Saint Louis Post-Dispatch. (November 17, 1978). Article on Page 56. Retrieved from https://www.newspapers.com/newspage/139164210/

Salley, P. (n.d.). Isis Theatre. Retrieved from Cinema Treasures, http://cinematreasures.org/theaters/1430

Sampson, W. (March 18, 2009). Walt's Return to Marceline 1956. *MousePlanet*. Retrieved from https://www.mouseplanet.com/8737/Walts_Return_to_Marceline_1956

Santa Barbara Biltmore (2017). Wikipedia entry. Retrieved from https://en.wikipedia.org/wiki/Santa_Barbara_Biltmore

Silvester, W. (2014). *The Adventures of Young Walt Disney*. Theme Park Press.

Smith, D. (2012). *Disney Trivia from the Vault: Secrets Revealed and Questions Answered*. Disney Editions: New York.

Smith, D. (2006). *The Official Encyclopedia Disney A to Z*. Third Edition. Disney Editions. New York.

Smith, D. (ed.) (1994). *Walt Disney Famous Quotes*. Kingdom Editions.

Smith, D. (n.d.). Ask Dave: Fred, Port Orange, Florida. Walt Disney Archives. Retrieved from https://d23.com/ask-dave/fred-port-orange-florida/

State University of New York (SUNY)-Fredonia. (n.d.). Disney Hall. Retrieved from fredonia.edu/reslife/disney.asp

Strand Theatre (Manhattan). (n.d.). Wikipedia entry. Retrieved from en.wikipedia.org/wiki/Strand_Theatre (Manhattan)

Stein, A. (July 5, 2012). Walt Disney spends a weekend at the Seattle World's Fair beginning on September 21, 1962. Retrieved from http://www.historylink.org/File/10142

Storytellers (Statue). Retrieved from https://en.wikipedia.org/wiki/Storytellers (statue)

Strodder, C. (2015). *The Disneyland Book of Lists*. Santa Monica Press: Santa Monica, CA.

Strutner, S. (January 27, 2017). Inside 21 Royal, Disneyland's New Hidden Dinner Experience That Costs $15,000. Retrieved from http://www.huffingtonpost.com/entry/21-royal-disneyland-restaurant_us_588b9730e4b08a14f7e5b574

Susanin, T. (2011). *Walt Before Mickey: Disney's Early Years, 1919-1928*. University Press of Mississippi: Jackson, MS.

Thankyouwaltdisney.org. (n.d.). Homepage. Retrieved from thankyouwaltdisney.org
This Day in Disney History (2017). May 9. Retrieved from
http://thisdayindisneyhistory.homestead.com/May09.html

This Fairytale Life (May 30, 2014). My Visit Inside Club 1901. Retrieved from
http://thisfairytalelife.com/visit-inside-club-1901/

Thomas, B. (1998). *Building a Company: Roy O. Disney and the Creation of an Entertainment Empire*. Hyperion: New York.

Thomas, B. (1994). *Walt Disney: An American Original*. Disney Editions.

Three Rivers Historical Museum. (2017). About Us. Retrieved from http://www.3rmuseum.org/about-us/

Titizian, J. (September 21, 2011). Recap: Our grandpa, Walt Disney. Retrieved from
https://www.waltdisney.org/blog/recap-our-grandpa-walt-disney

Today's Orlando. (2013). Walt Disney Amphitheater. Retrieved from
http://www.todaysorlando.com/thing-to-do/walt-disney-amphitheater

The Toluca Times. (January 27, 2010). The Sheri and Roy P. Disney Center for Integrative Medicine. Retrieved from tolucantimes.info/special_issues/beauty-health-fitness/the-sheri-and-roy-p-disney-center-for-integrative-medicine

U.S. Congress. (November 11, 2003). PUBLIC LAW 108–110. Retrieved from
https://www.congress.gov/108/plaws/publ110/PLAW-108publ110.pdf

Warner, J. (2014). Young Walt Disney: A Biography of Walt Disney's Younger years. Lifecaps.

Walt's Apartment (July 13, 2013). Walt and Lillian are married, July 13, 1925. Retrieved from
http://www.waltsapartment.com/walt-and-lillian-are-married-july-13-1925/

Walt Disney's Carousel of Progress (n.d.). Retrieved from
https://disneyworld.disney.go.com/attractions/magic-kingdom/walt-disney-carousel-of-progress/

Walt Disney's Original E.P.C.O.T. (n.d.). Introduction. Retrieved from
https://sites.google.com/site/theoriginalepcot/the-florida-project

Walt Disney Birthplace (May 10, 2016). Join Us for "Creativity Days" at the Walt Disney Birthplace This June! Retrieved from thewaltdisneybirthplace.org/2016/05/10/creativity-days-june-2016/

Walt Disney Birthplace (March 3, 2016). Disney Pledges $250,000 to The Walt Disney Birthplace. Retrieved from http://www.thewaltdisneybirthplace.org/2016/03/03/1466/

Walt Disney Birthplace (December 17, 2013). Like Father, Like Sons: Elias Disney, Entrepreneur. Retrieved from http://www.thewaltdisneybirthplace.org/2013/12/17/like-father-like-sons-elias-disney-entrepreneur/

Walt Disney Birthplace (n.d.). A Very Brief History of the House. Retrieved from
thewaltdisneybirthplace.org/

The Walt Disney Company (n.d.). *Walt Disney Archives Brochure*

The Walt Disney Company (2017). *Walt Disney Imagineering Fact Sheet.* Retrieved from https://aboutdisneyparks.com/about/around-the-world/walt-disney-imagineering

Walt Disney Concert Hall 10th Anniversary (2013). A Gift for the Phil. Retrieved from http://wdch10.laphil.com/wdch/vision.htm

Walt Disney Family Museum (WDFM). (2017). About the Museum. Retrieved from http://waltdisney.com/about/the-museum

Walt Disney Family Museum (WDFM). (August 6, 2016). *Walt and Sharon Take a Trip to Alaska.* Retrieved from http://www.waltdisney.org/blog/walt-and-sharon-take-trip-alaska

Walt Disney Family Museum (WDFM). (January 18, 2012). *New Heights: Walt and the Winter Olympics.* Retrieved from http://www.waltdisney.com/blog/new-heights-walt-and-winter-olympics

Walt Disney Family Museum (WDFM). (January 16, 2012). *New Heights: Mount Disney and Sugar Bowl.* Retrieved from http://waltdisney.org/blog/new-heights-mount-disney-and-sugar-bowl

Walt Disney Family Museum (WDFM). (n.d.). Home for the Holidays at Carolwood. Retrieved from http://waltdisney.org/HomeHolidays

Walt Disney Hometown Museum (WDHM). (2017a). Meet the Volunteers. Retrieved from https://www.waltdisneymuseum.org/visit-us/meet-the-volunteers/.

Walt Disney Hometown Museum (WDHM). (2017b). Disney Attractions. Retrieved from https://www.waltdisneymuseum.org/marceline/disney-attractions/.

Walt Disney Hometown Museum (WDHM). (2017c). Homepage. Retrieved from https://www.waltdisneymuseum.org/.

Walt Disney Hometown Museum (WDHM). (n.d.). Marceline: 100 Years of Disney History. Retrieved from waltdisneymuseum.org/wp-content/uploads/One-Hundred-Years-of-Disney-History-text.pdf

Walt Disney Magnet School. (2008). History. Retrieved from http://www.disney.cps.edu/history.html

Walt Disney Studios (n.d.). The Walt Disney Studios History. Retrieved from http://studioservices.go.com/disneystudios/history.html

Walt Disney World (n.d.a). Walt Disney World Railroad – Main Street, U.S.A. Retrieved from https://disneyworld.disney.go.com/attractions/magic-kingdom/walt-disney-world-railroad/

Walt Disney World (n.d.b). Walt Disney: Marceline to Magic Kingdom Tour. Retrieved from https://disneyworld.disney.go.com/events-tours/magic-kingdom/marceline-to-magic-kingdom/

Walt Disney World (April 30, 1969). *More than Three Years of Planning and Preparation Required before Construction of Walt Disney World.* Company News Release.

Watts, S. (1997). *The Magic Kingdom: Walt Disney and the American Way of Life.* Columbia, MO: University of Missouri Press.

WDW Radio (January 24, 2013). Hidden Walt Disney Tribute at Disney's Hollywood Studios in World Disney World. Retrieved from https://www.youtube.com/watch/?v=Wxh5Txg9yEE

Wednesday with Walt: A Disney Love Story. (July 13, 2011). Chip & Company. Retrieved from http://www.chipandco.com/wednesday-with-walt-a-disney-love-story-37505/

Weed, A. (December 3, 2013). *Wine Spectator.* Silverado Vineyards Cofounder Diane Disney Miller Dies. Retrieved from winespectator.com/webfeature/show/id/49343

Weiss, W. (April 4, 2014). Walt Disney Elementary School in Marceline, Missouri. Missouriland at Yesterland. Retrieved from yesterland.com/wdschool.html

Weiss, W. (December 5, 2008). Walt Disney in Chicago. Retrieved from http://www.yesterland.com/waltchicago.html

What is DeMolay? (2017). Retrieved from https://demolay.org/what-is-demolay/

Winton, M. (March 28, 2015). Walt Disney Related Portland Oregon Connection. YouTube Video. Retrieved from https://www.youtube.com/watch?v=3Rxij2yrUH8&hd=1

Young, J. (January 31, 2009). LAistory: Carthay Circle Theatre. Laist. Retrieved from http://laist.com/2009/01/31/laistory_carthay_circle_theater.php

Index

375

376

377

383

"...Disneyland will never be finished.
It's something we can keep
developing and adding to..."
-Walt Disney

"Walt's Pilgrimage will never been finished.
It will continue to evolve
as we discover more places
in Walt Disney's life."
-Christopher W. Tremblay

About the Author

Dr. Christopher W. Tremblay is a graduate of the Western Michigan University Lee Honors College and has been fascinated by Disney since his parents took him to Walt Disney World when he was 5. During his undergraduate studies, Tremblay participated in the Walt Disney World College Program (WDWCP), where he spent a semester learning all about the Disney enterprise and earned his "Ducktorate Degree" and the Rachel Imilio Scholarship for designing a new theme park called "Downtown Disney." That's also when he received his first set of mouse ears and met Dick Nunis (see photo below). On the WDWCP, he earned the nickname of "Mr. Pixie Dust." One of Tremblay's undergraduate honors courses was "American Pop Culture," and in that class he wrote about the cultural impact of the opening of Disneyland in 1955. Tremblay's honors college thesis was entitled, "Promoting Square Feet with Character: The Influence of Fantasy on Meetings and Conventions at Walt Disney World." In 2015, Tremblay developed and first taught "Walt's Pilgrimage," a course in the Study in the States Program for students enrolled in the Lee Honors College at Western Michigan University. He is a member of the Disney

College Program Alumni Association and a shareholder of The Walt Disney Company. Tremblay has supported The Walt Disney Birthplace and has a brick at the Walt Disney Hometown Museum and in front of the Magic Kingdom at Walt Disney World's "Walk Around the World." Tremblay is also the author of article entitled, "Disney for Credit: The Presence of Disney in the Academy." He earned his Doctor of Education degree from the University of Michigan-Dearborn. Tremblay lives in Michigan. This is the first book he has authored. Contact Tremblay at waltspilgrimage@gmail.com.

Tremblay is available for college course development, consulting, and trip planning. He has organized four "Walt's Pilgrimage" college courses for Western Michigan University's Lee Honors College and more are in the works.

facebook.com/waltspilgrimage

Photo with Mickey by the Walt Disney World College Program.
Photo of Tremblay by Mike Lanka of Lanka Photography. Used with permission.
Photo with Dick Nunis by the Walt Disney World College Program.

waltspilgrimage.com

Check out Tremblay's other Disney book:

Walt's Pilgrimage Jr.
A children's book that highlights
some of the major cities in Walt Disney's life.

In the works:

Walt of the Day
A daily walk through of Walt's life

Walt's Suitcase
A trivia book based on facts revealed in Walt's Pilgrimage

In the future:
Walt's Pilgrimage
International Edition
A second edition covering South America, Europe, and more.

Made in the USA
Monee, IL
10 January 2021